Tower Hill/zion u m w
Christian Personhood
1993

Secrets from Ordinary Places

Other Books by Ruth Senter

Startled by Silence
  Finding God in Unexpected Places
Surrounded by Mystery
  Finding God in the Contradictions of Faith
The Secrets of Friendship
So You're a Pastor's Wife

Secrets from Ordinary Places

*Finding God
In the
Every Day*

RUTH SENTER

Zondervan Publishing House
Grand Rapids, Michigan

Secrets from Ordinary Places
Copyright © 1990 by Ruth Senter

This is a Daybreak Book
Published by the Zondervan Publishing House
1415 Lake Drive, S.E., Grand Rapids, Michigan 49506

Library of Congress Cataloging-in-Publication Data

Senter, Ruth Hollinger, 1944–
    Secrets from ordinary places / Ruth Senter.
        p.   cm.
    ISBN 0-310-52971-9
    1. Meditations. 2. Christian life—1960– I. Title.
    BV4832.2.S44   1990
    242—dc20   90–37889
                                                                      CIP

All Scripture quotations, unless otherwise noted, are taken from the HOLY BIBLE: NEW INTERNATIONAL VERSION (North American Edition). Copyright © 1973, 1978, 1984, by the International Bible Society. Used by permission of Zondervan Bible Publishers.

Printed in the United States of America

90 91 92 93 94 95 / ML / 10 9 8 7 6 5 4 3 2 1

"Look to this day for yesterday is already a dream, and tomorrow is only a vision. But today well lived makes every yesterday a dream of happiness and every tomorrow a vision of hope. Look well therefore to this day. Such is the salutation of the dawn."

An old Indian Proverb

Contents

PART III: FINDING GOD THROUGH EMOTIONS

The Splendor
of the Ordinary

Graduation day was all the mother of the graduate could wish it to be. For weeks we had anticipated the grand celebration. The morning dawned crisp, cool, and sunny—custom-made for "Pomp and Circumstance." I was the typical mother who reached for the Kleenex as the long maroon and white procession started down the aisle, and I suddenly realized—a little girl is grown.

Our row of chairs was filled with aunts, uncles, cousins, and grandparents. We laughed, cried, and stretched high in our seats to see over the heads to view the only face in the crowd that mattered—our graduate. We were proud. We clicked our cameras, waved our programs, and smiled from ear to ear. It was a moment to be caught, captured, and enshrined forever.

The party actually had started three days earlier when the first out-of-town relatives arrived at the airport. The house was spotless, and the refrigerator was filled with a grand assortment of food to accompany the celebration. Gifts arrived in the mail, phone calls came from relatives in distant states, and friends and neighbors dropped in to add their congratulations. It was a jubilant time—like a few others we had known.

I wanted to stop the clock, but all too soon we were making the return trip to the airport, waving good-bye, cleaning up the crumbs under the dining room table, and throwing away the wrinkled bows and wrapping paper. I washed the last dish, watched the video of the graduation ceremony for one last time, and suddenly, life was ordinary again. I fed the cat, watered my geraniums on the front porch, then sat down and listened to the stillness of the house. Everyone had gone. I was alone with the reality that things would never be the same.

I sat the next morning and wrote my thoughts. I grieved for the high schooler I no longer had, I grieved for the finality of carefree youth (tomorrow she would start her job as security guard on the evening shift of a large corporation nearby), but also I grieved for the celebration that was no more.

Life contains emotional peaks where I wish I could sit forever. I anticipate, I savor, and when I have to leave the heights, I grieve. I would much rather celebrate than clean up the garage or wash the dirty dishes in the sink. But life hands me unadorned days filled with functional routine. Balloons and streamers and gaily wrapped packages are few and far between. Staleness threatens, like the dull, dry days of August when the air conditioner hums all day, and the Kool-Aid keeps disappearing from the refrigerator, and the mailman brings nothing but pizza coupons and an advertisement for a sale at the hardware store.

Life sometimes feels anemic compared to the fantasy that flashes on screens before me, or the life I suppose my neighbor to live when she tells me of her golf outing to Palm Springs or her ski trip to Tahoe.

Most mornings, I do not jump enthusiastically out of bed to exciting, action-packed moments. Rather I push myself upward and outward, put one foot in front of the other, and set about to do what needs to be done—making breakfast, going to work, doing laundry, weeding the flower beds, answering correspondence, paying bills. Non-descript days. Ordinary moments. Life that can easily reduce itself to boredom unless I know how to wrap the ordinary moments with fresh meaning and purpose.

"Easier said than done," I say to myself when I wait for a freight train to pass or try to balance the checkbook. How does one go about transforming ordinary moments into meaningful celebrations of life? The place to begin is to accept the fact that most of life *is* ordinary. For a day is not ordinary or extra-ordinary in itself. It is ordinary or extra-ordinary depending on how I view it and what I choose to do with it.

Author Tom Howard captured the concept well in his book on the home entitled *Splendor in the Ordinary*. He did not write of splendid homes, rather of ordinary homes made splendid by the people who live and love and attach meaning to them.

If I would wrap the ordinary moments with meaning, I must learn to live in the present. Sadly, most of us live a step ahead of ourselves, always thinking about plans, goals, dreams, and tomorrow's schedules. Today slips by, and suddenly the moments are gone, without our having noticed them. The old Latin imperative often used by time-management experts, "Carpe Diem" (seize the day), is all too often forgotten. Rather than seizing the day, we let it slip through our fingers, lost for lack of interest.

I have never forgotten the old Indian proverb that hung on the wall of our home when I was growing up. In the picture an Indian stood by his canoe, looking out over a peaceful lake as the sun rose in the east. The motto read, "Look to this day. For yesterday is already a dream, and tomorrow is only a vision. But today well lived makes every yesterday a dream of happiness and every tomorrow a vision of hope. Look well therefore to this day. Such is the salutation of the dawn."

If I would "look well . . . to this day," I must learn the

power of observation. How does the wind feel in my face as I take my morning walk along Klein Creek? How high is the water under the bridge. What stage are the crab apple blossoms in? How did my neighbor look today when I passed her on the path? What did my son do when his good friend called and canceled the overnight they had planned? What song is the ice cream truck playing today when it makes its rounds through the neighborhood?

Such trivia *is* the "stuff" of life. For God often chooses to house his grandest secrets in bushes that burn on a desert floor (Exod. 3) and babies that cry in a drafty cow barn (Luke 2). His word to Elijah came not through the wind, the fire, or the earthquake, but in a "gentle whisper" (1 Kings 19).

If I would see God in the bush, the drafty cow barn, hear the gentle whisper, I must ever be on the lookout. He comes in surprising ways and unpredictable places. "You will seek me and find me when you seek me with all your heart," was God's promise to wayward Israel (Jer. 29:13). While the context of Jeremiah is rebellion, God's principle is the same for everyday living. If I would see God in the ordinary moments of my day, I must look for him. I must be always examining, always expecting, always reflecting.

Several years ago, on a family vacation to the Southeast, we were driving on a desolate stretch of Kentucky interstate when the gas gauge pointed to empty. It was not the time to be choosy about which gas station we picked for our fill-up. Gas stations were few and far between. I was relieved to see the sign announcing a truck stop two miles ahead, but I was not prepared for the dirt, dust, lines of eighteen-wheelers, and conclaves of men who hung around the pumps and talked in coded CB language. I had a choice—to stay in the clean, secure car with my doors tightly locked, or to join my family for a stretch and a walk into the restaurant. I decided to go with them, determined not to touch anything, eat anything, or get myself dirty.

As I browsed among the stacks of rearview mirrors, CB antennas, and brake fluid, I spotted a large cardboard box with "England" stamped on the side. I was immediately attracted by the incongruity of English imports in a greasy-spoon truck-stop restaurant. The box was filled with brown tissue paper. But wrapped in the brown tissue paper were delicate blue and white porcelain ducks, hearts, and rocking horses. They were the same porcelain window hangings I'd seen in country gift shops in some of the nicer shopping districts back home—for *half* the price.

I left the truck stop with three porcelain pieces, wrapped in brown lunch bags. But I ended up with more than country window hangings. I carried from that place a fresh lesson—sometimes life's greatest treasures come in ways we least expect. An ordinary to sub-ordinary truck stop? It could have been had I chosen to sit in the safety and cleanliness of the car. But moments embraced are often moments transformed. And in the transformation, I come away with the treasure.

If I am to see God in the ordinary events of my life, I must learn flexibility. Schedules, as useful as they are, may well be God's greatest obstacle when he seeks our attention. I zoom through my day, bent on keeping my schedule and fulfilling my responsibilities, never willing to flex for lessons close at hand. I have plans for my day. Sometimes God speaks through interruptions. I have productivity in mind. Sometimes God's voice comes only in stillness. I prefer familiarity. Sometimes God comes in unfamiliar guise. Sometimes seeing God in the ordinary moments of my day means surrendering my schedule to make room for him.

Gladys Aylward was an English missionary to China in the 1940s. In a poignant scene from the movie "The Inn of Sixth Happiness," which chronicles her life, the emperor Chin Song is speaking to an English lieutenant who has fallen in love with Gladys but is reluctant to admit it for fear of disrupting his career. "A life that is planned is a closed life, my friend," says the emperor. "It can be endured, perhaps. It cannot be lived."

So it is with ordinary moments. Tightly controlled, functionally precise, they may well remain ordinary moments that grow stale and meaningless. How tragic if life should become nothing more than what T.S. Eliot describes in his poem "The Love Song of J. Alfred Prufrock." Prufrock reflects, "I've measured out my life in coffee spoons." Measured out in coffee spoons, given gingerly and stingily, life becomes a meaningless rut. Given in joyful abandonment, ordinary moments become stepping-stones to growth and discovery.

If I would transform insignificant routine into significant reminders of God's presence, I must learn contentment. I have only the moments God has given *me*. I cannot live another's. And yet how easy to focus on the moments he has given others—their opportunities, their gifts, their lifestyles. I cannot see the green grass under my feet if I am always looking at the greener grass under another's feet. Likewise, I do not hear God's voice when I am always wondering what he is saying to another. How often I forfeit a fresh glimpse of God because my sights are on what God is doing in or for another, rather than on what he might be doing for me, right here in my ordinary time and place.

Oswald Chambers, in his devotional classic *My Utmost for His Highest*, has said, "Staleness is an indication of something out of joint with God." When it comes to ordinary moments, I have a choice. Either I can redeem them for God or I can settle into staleness, distance myself from the gentle whispers of God, so that all I have left from a day is trivia to record in a two-dollar spiral notebook, or pages left blank for lack of significant entry. But moments redeemed—ordinary moments infused with the voice and presence of God—fill the page, add depth, beauty, and joy to my days. "Look well therefore to this day, for such is the salutation of the dawn."

PART I: FINDING GOD THROUGH OTHER PEOPLE

CHAPTER ONE

Secrets of Being Loved

Musing from an Interstate

I watch him from the tollbooth
He sits by the interstate
Without even a sign to Pittsburgh or New York City
Bound for nowhere, I suppose
His life contained
In a small canvas bag
Matched luggage to the weeds
Brown weeds
Brittle weeds
Weeds growing nowhere
Using up space beside the interstate.
It doesn't matter that they grow.
They are part of
No one's plan.
Here today
Gone tomorrow.
But the traveler is not so.
His soul is not so easily disposed.
God
Remembers that he sits beside the interstate
Without even a sign to Pittsburgh or New York City.
He is bound for somewhere
God knows where.
For
God
Loves who he is
Cares about where he is
Believes in what he could be.

Lord,
For those who
Sit by the interstate
Keeping company with the weeds
May I
Love who they are
Care about where they are
Believe in what they could be
Because it's what you've done for me.

"We Belong Together, Don't We?"

I suppose I am most easily led when I'm not aware I'm being led. Maybe we are all that way. This morning I am led by a child, who sits beside me in the back seat of the car as we drive through the quiet Pennsylvania morning on our way to some insignificant errand.

"I'll go get it," I had volunteered when the need arose. "Oh, can I go with Aunt Ruth?" Naphatali had piped up from in front of the bay window of Grandma's big, old white house on the hill. She was deeply absorbed in her favorite pastime—coloring a picture for some aunt, uncle, cousin, or for Grandma's refrigerator door. But even favorite pastimes paled in significance to being with one of the twenty-one aunts, uncles, cousins, grandmas or grandpas who gathered in Grandma's house during four days of family reunion. With all the gusto of a six year old, she quickly laid aside her colors, grabbed her coat, and headed for the car before we had finalized who was coming along.

"Oh, I might as well ride along with you," my brother Denny said from behind the sports page. "It's a nice morning for a drive. We can take my car."

"I was thinking the same thing about a nice morning for a drive." My mother's voice came from the kitchen, where she was drying the breakfast dishes. "Mind if I ride along, too?"

With twenty-one people in the house, the four of us would barely be missed, but I did think to myself as we piled into the car, *What started as a solo mission has turned into a pleasant carful.*

My niece caught my mood. "Isn't this fun, Aunt Ruth?" Her dark eyes shone as she locked her seat belt, eagerly ready for a ride with her family.

Perhaps it was the day—a balmy sixty-five degrees, in December. Perhaps it was the early morning mist, which turned the rolling hills to gold. Perhaps it was the peaceful pastures of sheep and cows, even a few solitary hens. Maybe Naphatali was celebrating her ten-day holiday from school or Grandma's steaming Moravian sugar cake that she had eaten for breakfast. There were many possible reasons why a six-year-old's eyes might shine on this particular Wednesday in December.

We accomplished our mission. We'd poked through "The Tin Bin," found the part we needed for hanging Grandma's new tin lamp over the kitchen table, and then headed home. Naphatali's obvious joy seemed complete. She sighed a long, satisfied sigh, squeezed my hand, and said, "Aunt Ruth. Isn't this neat. We all belong together.

You're my aunt. Daddy is your brother. Grandma is your mother. Everybody in this car goes together."

I squeezed her hand and smiled as I looked into her shining eyes. "Yes, Naphatali, this is neat. We *do* belong together."

I have thought often of Naphatali's simple celebration of family. When I am tempted to "do it on my own," or bury myself in my favorite pastime, I remember her dark eyes shining with the childlike awe of belonging to someone other than herself. In those moments of remembering, I am warmed by a sense of belonging together.

Miracle in Trafalgar Square

This evening as I listen to my daughter's voice, I think to myself, *Eighteen years old seems awfully young and London, England, seems awfully far away.* "You're touring London by yourself?" I try not to register the concern I feel. "Couldn't you find someone to go with you?"

Jori's voice is calmly confident. "Everyone else is busy. It's the only day I have to see London. I'll be all right, Mom."

I'm not convinced. Most big cities I know of, even closer to home, offer challenges enough for any adult, let alone a teenager. And this city is not only far away, but unknown to me.

"Well, do be careful," I caution with motherly protection. As I hang up the phone, I feel the bittersweet transition pains from being the mother of a child to being the mother of an adult. *Where did the years go?* I ask myself.

I have never been the mother of an adult before. Now I feel anxious. I have never had to practice faith with a child 4,000 plus miles away from home. "Do not let not your hearts be troubled and do not be afraid" (John 14:27), seems to work much better for me when my children are under my roof.

On Wednesday, Jori visits London. She moves in and out of my anxious thoughts all day. I pray for her safety, not thinking to pray for anything more.

Early Friday morning, I am awakened by the phone's ringing. I hear Jori's excited voice on the other end, "Mother. Sit down. Do you want to hear a story?"

I sit down and brace myself for the worst. Her voice sounds normal, so I know she is okay. Her words come rushing and tumbling over each other as she describes Trafalgar Square, filled with hundreds of people. On this bright spring noon, Jori paused to rest on a park bench, wistfully thinking that it would be nice to have a companion for the second half of the day. Not one to dwell on what she does not have, Jori was just ready to press on to the next point of interest when a stranger from the crowd, "a pleasant looking girl about my age," she said on the phone, "sat down beside me."

"Are you seeing London by yourself?" she asked Jori, "I am too. How about spending the rest of the afternoon together."

As they began their walk, the miracle unfolded. "What are you doing in London?" Jori asked.

"Well, I've just been to a Torchbearer Bible School in Sweden, and I'm on my way to its sister school in northern England."

There, in the middle of Trafalgar Square, Jori threw her arms around her new-found friend and cried for joy. "I've just been to a Torchbearer Bible School in Germany, and I'm on my way to the Bible School in northern England too!"

I cry tears of thankfulness as I sit here at my desk in the 2 A.M. morning hours, listening to the good news.

"Now, mother, God still does miracles, doesn't he?" Jori asked.

"Yes, he does Jori," I say through my tears. "And I imagine God might have been up there in heaven, looking down on Trafalgar Square and saying to himself, *There's a little lonely girl from Illinois down there who needs a friend. Let me remind her how big I really am.*

I return to bed, wiping away my tears, convinced that it was really Jori's mother who needed the reminder of how big her God really is, even with her child-adult so far away from home.

Pete's Place

 I am generally not choosy about who works on my car. If a mechanic knows what to do about the whirring noises coming from my engine, who cares if he has dirt under his fingernails, or that his hair is shoulder length and looks like it hasn't been washed for two weeks.

At least that's how I thought I would feel. But today, riding cold on the heels of one of Chicago's most bitter winter chills, I am brought face to face with my preconceived notions about what is and what is not acceptable, even when it comes to the person who works on my car.

I am about three miles from home when a strange knocking sound begins in my motor. It is not the day to be taking risks with my car. The thermometer outside the kitchen window read -20 below at 6 A.M. when I first ventured a look. I do not relish a walk in the frozen tundra. Fortunately, I am almost directly in front of our local gas station when the strange noises begin.

Fine folks they are, these people at the gas station, I think to myself. I have done small business with them before. The station is clean and litter free; the help are neatly uniformed with wide, white smiles, like the station attendants you once saw in the Texaco commercials on television. I have no second thoughts as I turn my Pontiac 6000 into their driveway, find an attendant, and explain my dilemma.

"Sorry, lady. We are booked for the next month and a half. With all this below zero weather, it's been a zoo around here."

I think perhaps he has misunderstood. I repeat my request to have him simply look under my hood and tell me whether my car is driveable.

"I can't take a chance in having to walk home in this kind of weather. . . ." I think perhaps an appeal to his emotions will work. He remains unbending.

"Sorry lady, there are twenty-five people with cars waiting before you. Everyone thinks their situation is an emergency. . . ."

I am left with one other option—Pete's place. It used to be my kind of place. Pete was our mechanic for years. Trusted. True. Dependable. And neat. Yes, neat. Every tool in its proper place. Not a trace of grease or dirt on his hands or uniform. And he even wore white shirts to work. Pete was a member of our church, and I liked his way of conducting business.

I had watched sadly as Pete sold his business and moved South. His once neat, well-kept garage looked more like a junkyard now that there were new owners. Today I knew I had no other choice. Pete's place was just around the corner.

I took a deep breath and pushed open the door. A very large man with a stocking cap pulled down over his face sat leaning against the wall, apparently taking an early morning siesta. Dirty rags, piles of auto parts, tools, tires, and various strange shapes and sizes littered the room. A man with long blond hair and a dangling earring in one ear stood behind the counter chewing on the end of a pencil.

I wanted to run from this place but the thought of walking home in sub-zero weather forced the words out of my mouth. "Could you please look under my hood and tell me about the knocking noise."

The man with the dangling earring put down his pencil and sprang into action. "Be happy to, ma'am. Pull her right in here." And with that the large garage doors opened and I drove in among the canyon of junk.

The sleeping señor awoke from his siesta, pulled his stocking cap from over his face, and lumbered over to a thermos of coffee. "Care for some coffee as you wait?" he asked with all the sincerity of a country gentleman.

An hour later, I'd forgotten the context. I'd been taken in by the care. The silver-earringed man had explained everything as he went along, and the sleepy señor had served me coffee twice.

"It's not fixed permanently, Mrs. Senter. But it will get you home without blowing the engine. Now you just forget the pay. Glad I could help you." The mechanic slammed the hood, and as I left, I noticed the other man was back in his corner asleep again with his stocking cap back over his face.

Once safely home, I reflected on the junk-heap garage, the dangling-earringed mechanic, and the sleeping coffee-man. *I was a stranger and they took me in.* And what an interesting twist that I should be taken in by those I considered "not my kind." Perhaps angels of mercy sometimes come dressed in different guise, so we can realize how blinding stereotypes can really be.

Sometimes Gentle Men Die Violent Deaths

He was a gentle man in every sense of the word. His was a powerful, quiet presence I felt as he walked through the halls at church on Sunday mornings. He always stopped to greet me, as though I were the only person around. His "Good Morning" rang true because it was true. For him, life itself was a "Good Morning." I sensed it from the look of contentment on his face.

Today, I sit here with his friends gathered in this sanctuary to remember the good mornings, the good evenings, the good days he lived. Those who knew him best recall the gentle man that he was—the father who knelt on the floor and taught his two young sons to use a jigsaw on boards; the third-grade boys' Sunday school teacher, who volunteered every year for jobs no one else wanted to do in the Sunday school Christmas program; the friend who came alongside a struggling brother, week after week, entering where no one else dared tread; the neighbor who walked his street with the garbage man, helping to lift the cans because "garbage men need to feel special, too"; the public servant whose daily work made life better for thousands of children across the state.

Gentle men shouldn't die so soon, I keep thinking. They are the genuine kind who restore our faith in this fallen lot. They are the solid kind who remind us of why we are here and what service is all about. They are the quiet kind who convict and convince you that what you are is far more important than what you do, that quality of life far surpasses quantity of life.

This gentle man lived but thirty-eight short years. And when we heard the news that he'd been shot, we shook our heads; our hearts melted. Gentle men don't die so soon. They aren't gunned down by the very person they were praying for. They don't write in their spiritual journal one day about doing their Father's will and the next day give away their blood behind their desk at work.

Oh, but gentle men do die violent deaths. Jesus knelt with little children and taught them lessons. He walked alongside struggling brothers and healed them without fanfare or reward. He made the woman at the well feel special with new life. And when it came his time to die, he prayed for those who took his life, "Father forgive them, for they do not know not what they are doing" (Luke 23:34). And then the gentlest of all men bowed his head and died.

Yes, sometimes gentle men do die violent deaths, I think to myself. Lord, may I learn from their gentleness.

Andy

If you asked him, Andy might not even be able to explain to you the doctrine of the Holy Spirit. As a sophomore in high school, handsome basketball star, male lead in the all-school musical, he has probably not given the topic much thought. But on that rainy Easter Sunday in Kentucky, Andy taught me a lesson about the Holy Spirit I will never forget.

"Mrs. Senter. Would you come check Rich? He's not feeling well and he looks kinda funny," a member of the bass section called out to me as we loaded the Greyhound bus for the final leg of our ten-day high-school choir tour. We had climbed the granite stone mountain outside of Atlanta, Georgia, surfed the waves on Florida's west coast, and sang against the backdrop of Disney World's Magic Kingdom—all with nothing more than a few minor sore throats and upset stomachs. As one of the choir parents for fifty-three high schoolers, today I was beginning to breathe easily. It was our last day out and home was in sight. The kids were tired but safe and well, and basically in good spirits. So far, there had been nothing my mothering skills had not been able to handle.

Now, as I caught sight of Rich's face, my maternal confidence took a sudden dip. Apart from a five-minute crash course on what to do in case of insulin reaction, offered by the mother of one of our diabetics five minutes before we boarded the bus, I knew nothing about the care and treatment of diabetics, much less what to do when one needs food to keep himself in balance but has not been able to keep anything down for the past three hours. Instantly I knew I was looking at a potential crisis. Rich shook. His face was flushed red, and his eyes were fixed on some far-away point. I was not even sure he saw me.

"Rich. Rich. Talk to me. When did you last have your insulin?" His eyes roamed their sockets, as though he could not gather his thoughts together long enough to collect the answer.

I grabbed a sleeping bag and pillow with one thought on my mind. *Andy.* Andy was the other diabetic on tour, and he would know what to do. I yelled his name, apparently with the kind of vibrations that sent bodies scurrying. Andy was beside me in an instant.

"Stay calm, Mrs. Senter. I know what to do." He knelt beside Rich and opened his emergency insulin kit. I hovered over the proceedings—alarmed, helpless, ignorant, having nothing to offer but my presence. Andy worked quickly and confidently, assuring me as he went along. "He'll be all right, Mrs. Senter. He'll be all right. We just need to get something sweet from this tube into his mouth. Quick. Have someone run for a 7Up. Here, help me cover him up. Get me a granola bar too. We should try that for the fiber." ·

I followed orders, totally dependent on this high-school sophomore who had come alongside me in my helplessness. I pulled a blanket over the shaking boy while Andy gently forced sweetness into Rich's mouth. The color drained from Rich's face, but eventually the shaking stopped. His eyes closed. Andy took a quick sugar count, roused Rich from his sleep several times, then sat back on his heels and relaxed. I knew the crisis had passed.

The 6'2" basketball star rose to his feet and stood before me. Never have I had such a sense of someone moving in alongside of me to do for me what I could not do for myself. Andy had assured, comforted, instructed, and formed the petitions for me when I didn't even know how to ask. I reached out and gave him a big hug. As I did, I thought of what the Holy Spirit does for me each day of my life. He comes alongside and offers me enablement. Amazing how I struggle so to do on my own when he is there simply for the calling!

CHAPTER TWO

Secrets of Letting Go

The Rock

See this rock, Lord?
It is a rock of silence.
I have stood on this rock.
And shouted into the wind
To get Your attention.
But the currents of air
Have carried my prayers,
Dashed them against the cliffs
So that they come back to me
Like an echo
Across the valley
Empty words
Without response.

Now, Lord, I have a plan.
I will stand on this rock.
And as You come by,
Show me Your glory.
I am Moses, a mere man.
And a man can only take so much
Without visual assurances.
If I just see Your face,
Know You've heard,
See some signs of the changes
I desire.
I will have the courage to go on.

But
He did not show me His face.
"No one may see Me and live."
He did not bring the change
I so desired.
Instead,
He put me in the cleft of the rock
Covered me with His hand
While He passed by.
And I was left
With a view of God
From the backside
And a view of the Promised Land from far away.
I did not see the glory I requested.
But I was hidden in the rock.
And today I have known
God's care
In the midst of God's denial.

The Bittersweet of Letting Go

It is Sunday morning, early August, and the small congregation sings its worship and praise. I am bodily here, sitting in the pew, the wife of the visiting preacher. But mentally, I am four weeks down the road, walking an airport concourse with our eighteen-year-old daughter, who, with two large suitcases and a trunk, is bound for Zurich, Switzerland and college in Germany.

My mind fills itself with unknowns. Will I be calm for Jori on that day? Will I be able to maneuver past the lump in my throat to say one final "good-by"? Will I release her with confidence, knowing I have done my best for the last eighteen years, or will I return to the airport parking lot wishing I had done more?

The worship service progresses. We turn to hymn

number 256. I have sung Martin Luther's "A Mighty Fortress Is Our God" so often I don't even reach for the hymnal. We are into the last verse, and I haven't missed one syllable. Suddenly, I am no longer simply singing. I hear the words: "Let goods and kindred go. This mortal life also. The body they may kill. God's truth abideth still. His kingdom is forever."

I am struck with the thought that even great reformers of the faith must have struggled with surrender. For them, it was handing over their security, their positions, even their physical safety. My struggle today is of far lesser consequence than the one Martin Luther faced when he posted his ninety-five theses on the church door in Wittenberg, Germany. But whether it be releasing your firstborn to her college years or giving up personal safety, relinquishment is perhaps the most demanding of all commitments.

It is demanding because it runs head on into my self-centeredness. Relinquishment calls for a reversal of my natural bent. It means I must be willing to live without some one, some thing, some status, some right, some security. No wonder when Jesus talked about "losing one's life" as a guarantee for "saving it" (Matt. 16:25), his disciples did not understand. Such reasoning ran contrary to their natural way of thinking.

Sooner or later, life sees to it that we hand over something we hold dear. We lose a loved one through death. Our married children move across the nation. Our oldest child leaves for college. A daughter strays from the fold. We grit our teeth, sit out the pain, and resign ourselves to the unseen plan that we have no control over and would not have approved if we'd been given the choice. We are resigned to our "fate," but we do not know relinquishment. Relinquishment leads to peace. Resignation—"there is nothing I can do about it"—usually leads to bitterness, anger, and resentment.

Relinquishment is an acknowledgment that life will be filled with gifts and deprivations. It is giving mental assent to the fact that God has the right to give and to take. Things, people, positions, experiences, successes, securities, and joys will come and go. Relinquishment simply means that when it is time for them to go, I do not clutch because I have spent a lifetime holding them loosely. Job, the Old Testament man of suffering, exemplified relinquishment when, upon learning he had lost all his earthly possessions, including his children, he responded, "The LORD gave and the LORD has taken away; may the name of the LORD be praised" (Job 1:21).

It would be nice if in one grand act of commitment we settled forever the issue of giving up. While conversion itself demands no less than giving our all, we spend a lifetime working out the implications of our initial act of surrender. J. Wallace Hamilton, in his book *Ride the Wild Horses*, says, "Life is an unending exchange of material we can't keep for riches we can't lose. The willingness to exchange is the ultimate test of life."

Today, as my daughter packs her bags for college, I am faced with options. I can tighten my grasp. I have given my life to God, but, thank you, I will keep my daughter. I can choose to possess her, to question her decisions, to instruct her in all the areas I've forgotten during the past eighteen years, to force commitments and promises from her, to worry over her safety, to demand her itinerary, to talk her into staying close to home.

Or, I can choose to let her go—to keep my mouth shut, even though I feel like asking questions or providing input. I can choose to pray for her safety and then go to sleep instead of fantasizing danger. I can express my love to her, make myself available, but give her the space, time, and distance an eighteen-year-old needs and deserves.

In short, while I surrendered my life to God as a teen, each new day calls for new surrenders. Every day I stake my claims. But every day I must pull up those stakes and give God his rightful place as controller of my life. Each day fills my hands with new experiences, new opportunities, new possessions, new people (even those I know the best are never the same person twice). Each day I must resurrender them to God. Relinquishment does not stop with conversion. It only begins there.

But still, sometimes I go to bed at night, stare into the darkness, and picture the dangers that surround my children, my husband, my aging parents, my financial security. It is at such times I must relinquish my fears as well as my treasures.

Mentally, I walk with a young Hebrew mother who carries her eighteen-month-old to a river bank. We push past the cattails and reeds, stop and look out over alligator-infested waters. In an act of surrender, I tuck my own treasure into a tiny basket made of tar and pitch. With tears in my eyes and a lump in my throat, I push that basket out into the mercy of the Nile.

"But the waters are getting rough, Lord. And what about the alligators? I think I see one." I am ready to jump into a lifeboat and attempt a rescue. But such is not the way of relinquishment. Relinquishment stands by the riverbank, secure in the knowledge that there is a plan.

I must rest in the plan, even though there appears no rhyme or reason to murky, dangerous rivers. I must allow the waters to carry my treasure wherever God would send it. Being at peace with an uncertain outcome is one of the marks of relinquishment. I stand by the river. Pray by the river. But I do not try to rescue or repossess. In my night of unrest, I am reminded by a young Hebrew mother of what relinquishment is all about.

Sometimes relinquishment means giving up a cherished dream, a plan, an illusion. Life is often a series of adjustments—fitting our dreams to reality. I have my notions of what life should be. Unfortunately, my notions are sometimes more typical of paradise than of the cracked utopia in which I live. For some of us, relinquishment comes when we surrender our fantasies. I may never shake the world with great accomplishments by the time I'm fifty years old. Not every day will be peaceful. Not everyone will love me. People will make mistakes or disappoint me. Goals may rot on my journal page. Projections fall far short.

If I would know relinquishment, I must bring my illusions to the cross. I must hang them there and return to a world full of miscalculated projections. The cross reminds me that I do not need a perfect world where dreams always come true, but that in the midst of shattered hopes and drowned illusions, there is triumph. The cross faced squarely into the realities of life. It points me in the same direction.

But how bleak life would be if I never fantasized about how things could be. Relinquishment does not mean I will never dream or hope. It simply means if I have walked with God and given life my best efforts, I do not need a dream world in order to be at peace. I do not have to shake the world by age fifty. Sometimes, it may be OK simply to wash the dishes, play Monopoly with my fourteen-year-old, weed the garden, and write out the college tuition check each month. If the plan includes my dreams and hopes and wishes, I gratefully accept. But if not, I am still able to sing my song of thanksgiving with Moses who had just learned he would never enter the Promised Land (Deut. 32).

When all is said and done, relinquishment comes down to childlike faith in God as the ultimate keeper of our treasures. In the face of his own death, the apostle Paul wrote, "I know whom I have believed, and am convinced that he is able to guard what I have entrusted to him for that day" (2 Tim. 1:12)).

Our son Nicky was only three when he accompanied me one day to the local savings and loan. I stood at the teller's window ready to deposit a $100 bill into our savings account when I happened to glance down at Nicky and saw his little face wrinkled with concern. "Mommy, why are you giving that man our money?" his voice quivered.

The wise bank teller quickly zeroed in on my dilemma, leaned over the counter, and said, "Son, how would you like to see what I'm going to do with your money?"

The three of us wound our way down the curved staircase of the savings and loan and stopped before the massive two-ton doors that opened into the vault. "See these heavy doors, son, those steel drawers, and thick bars? They will lock tonight, and only a special electronic clock can open them in the morning. Your money will be safe because I will put it in this vault."

I could almost hear Nick's sigh of relief as he took my hand, went back upstairs, and watched in peace as I handed my $100 to the man on the other side of the counter. Our money was safe. Nicky had seen the vault, met the keeper of our funds.

Daily I am faced with the call to hand over my treasures. Often my face is etched with concern, and I clutch my $100 bill in fear of the unknown. But when I step back, take a look at those massive doors and thick steel bars, I can relax. God is the keeper of the vault, and *God can be trusted.* I don't need to stand guard by the treasury door. I can leave my valuables with God and be at peace.

Of Bedtimes and Final Term Papers

As one who sometimes takes life in a series of last-minute dashes for the finish line, I am prone to talk often to my children about the hardships of procrastination. I have memorized the lecture, stored it in my brain for handy, spur-of-the-moment retrieval.

I am tempted to pull it out tonight as I see one of my own sit down to yet another of life's last minute scrambles toward tomorrow's deadline. It is late—too late to be starting an English paper assigned a month ago. It is late— too late for mother to be worrying about her child's morning deadline. I skip the lecture and opt for bed instead, more out of tiredness than out of conviction. I am most often full of lectures at times like this, more often than I wish.

I climb into bed and stare into the darkness, serenaded by the click of the word processor. I think about my tiredness. Suddenly I think about her tiredness. Yes, the paper should have been started earlier, but she has not been sitting idly by—after-school job, yearbook meetings, choir concerts, a whirl of senior activities. I think to myself, *Excuses? I usually don't accept excuses. It is part of the real world to have more to do than moments in a day. How else will she learn responsibility?*

Nevertheless, I am drawn to the study where Jori sits hunched over a pile of books. Her eyes look dull, none of their usual sparkle. The wastebasket is full of discarded false starts, and a Coke that has long since lost its fizz sits half-finished on the desk. She chews on the end of a pencil and taps her fingers impatiently on the keyboard.

"Only three more pages to go, but I've run out of things to say. I know, I know . . . I should have started earlier when my brain was fresher. . . ."

I laugh at her paraphrase. She has heard the lecture enough times to commit it to memory, with slight variations along the way. "Now, isn't that what you were going to say?" She takes a sip of the flat Coke and grimaces at its taste.

"Not really. I've just come to sit in the study for a while. Nothing in particular." I plop down on the couch and pick up a book in which I have no interest. Mostly I've come just to sit near her. *Why am I sitting here?* I ask myself as the clock ticks toward midnight. *It is not my paper that is due at ten o'clock tomorrow. I am not the one who managed to let it go until the last minute.* However, I don't usually sit with my children while they write their term papers. But still I sit in silence, going through the motions of reading a book. I watch the occasional spurts of flurry over the keyboard and then hear long, deep groans and sighs, and yawns and periods of silent inactivity. It is clearly a night of torture for this senior English student. Toward the end I rub her back and ask if she might like another cold Coke.

"Oh, Mother, thanks." I hear her tearful voice. As I crawl back into bed, long past midnight, I think not so much about the completed English paper as about the One who comes and sits by my side, not in harsh judgment of my last-minute dashes, but in a silent companionship of love.

And I conclude that sometimes my children need for me to simply be with them. Life will deliver the lectures. Sometimes only a parent can sit with them in the hardships they have created for themselves, rub their backs, and refill their Coke that has long since lost its fizz.

Lessons from Closed Doors

His door is closed, painfully closed. I want to knock, to go in, to put my arms around my recently-turned-teenage son, and to tell him how sorry I am for our pain—my pain and his. But there is nothing I can do with this pain but let it be. It has come through his disobedience.

Nine o'clock sharp. I want you home, I remember my words. The parameters had been clearly defined. He even repeated my directive—no miscommunication here. I sit on the front porch swing and wait as daylight disappears and the lightning bugs begin their nocturnal fireworks. Nine o'clock comes and goes. I wait in agony through the next hour. I am uneasy, then angry, then thoughtfully resolute. I am now the administrator of justice because the terms have been ignored.

But there are plenty of reasons. He recites them to me one by one when he finally returns from his friend's house, almost an hour late. "I'm sorry, Mom. It really was a dumb thing to do, to ignore the clock. Next time I'll do better. I'll remember then." I think to myself, *He looks so sweet and innocent as he sits here before me with his sparkling blue eyes and his dimpled cheeks.*

I almost wink and say, "Okay, just this once, you may forget the rules." It would be so much easier that way, more peaceful for both of us, and we could still be friends. *After all, he is not the kind of kid who willfully disobeys. This is only a slight omission, a slip of the memory. Excusable. Pardonable.* Except for the rule: "Be home by nine." *What do I do with the rule?*

What did God do with the rules? He turned his back on his beloved Son because of broken rules. There was excruciating silence between Father and Son because justice had been offended, the laws ignored. Sin had to reap its awful consequences. The Son cried out, "My God, My God. Why have you forsaken me?" And on that painful day of retribution, Father and Son, though bonded in eternal love, knew severance and alienation because justice had to be done.

I know I cannot not wink at disobedience. I cannot teach my son that broken rules don't matter, so I pronounce the penalty. He walks to his room and closes his door. As a parent, one of God's representatives in our home, I must endure the temporary painful silences for a more enduring truth: My child will only understand sin as I teach him about consequences.

There is a gentle knock on my door. "Mom, can I come in?" He knows that tomorrow he will not participate in a baseball game with his friends, yet with sparkling blue eyes, he says, "Mom, I love you." Justice has been done; reconciliation is complete. He gives me a hug and kisses me good night.

Jori Doesn't Live Here Anymore

I walk tonight along the empty hall. Jori's room is dark and cold. It has been four months since my eighteen-year-old left for college—four months since this room has been warmed by her presence. I turn into the room, fumble for the light switch, and am stunned, as always, by the emptiness.

No music bounces from the walls. No voice purrs into the telephone or calls down the hall to see what time dinner will be ready. Cheerleading pom-poms hang mutely over the edge of her dresser and pictures stare in silent melancholy from the walls—moments of high school jubilation frozen in high speed ektachrome, captured between frames of flowers, hearts, and teddy bears.

I tell myself, *Jori doesn't live here anymore. This room is not her home.* I feel the emptiness inside me. I squeeze the teddy bear that sits forlornly at the head of her bed and run my hand over the soft white afghan she left folded neatly at the foot of her bed. She is a half a world away, attending school in Germany. The room is all I have of her for now. It is my link to her past.

I remember the days when I planned her life for her— birthday parties, picnics at the park, long hikes in the woods, ballet lessons, and fourth-grade field trips to Chicago's Art Institute. That was the way of childhood. Gradually, my plans gave way to hers. That was the way of growth. Now I praise her plans, marvel at her maturity, and cross the days off on the calendar until her return. For when I gave up a child, I also laid aside the right to plan for her. She will make her own decisions from now on— that's part of the price of giving up.

I remember her nearness. The nights she would crawl in bed beside me, frightened by the thunder that rattled her windows. Or, the long, cozy evenings she snuggled close while we pored through the pages of *Little House in the Big Woods* or *Charlotte's Web*. There were times she went out of her way to be close to me. When she walked past all others in a row, just to sit next to "Mommy," or the later years when she'd come home from a date, sit on the edge of my bed, and tell me about her evening.

But our nearness, our closeness was shattered—when the SwissAir 747 pulled away from the terminal, taxied down the runway, and took off into the sunset, bound for Zurich, Switzerland. I reached out and touched the cold glass windows that surrounded the gate area where we'd said our good-byes. It was the remainder of her touch—the only kind of touch I would know for a while—a touch of memory—things and places but not her.

Tonight as I stand at the window in her quiet room, I

see Christmas candles light the windows on our street. I celebrate the Christ child's birth, but I cry silently for my child whom I cannot touch. And I think that another time over a lonely stable, another parent wept for his absent child in another empty room—a celestial room. He, too, longed for nearness and perhaps even counted the empty years that lay ahead—thirty-three in all.

I walk out of Jori's room and turn through the empty hall. An absent child. That's the price of love. It is the message of Christmas. God loved so much that he gave up his child for me. This year I appreciate his gift in a new way.

I'll Do It Your Way

I double-check my list: Bible, note cards, schedule, watch. I am ready. I pull the back door closed behind me, fifteen minutes ahead of schedule. *Not bad for everything else I had to do this morning*, I think to myself as I leave to speak to a women's group. I am comfortable in my preparedness.

But then, I usually am prepared. I do not take assignments lightly. This morning is no exception. I have spent great time and energy thinking, praying, writing, outlining, building an introduction and conclusions, bridges and illustrations. I have the flow well in mind. Yes, I am ready.

I slip into the side room where the program committee has met early for prayer. I join the circle. As prayers continue, someone mentions the word *joy*. I think instantly of a story about joy and of how it would fit as my introduction. Except that I had not planned on telling that particular story. It would change my whole approach. Besides, if I changed my opening, I would need to change some of the Scripture references. And if I changed the Scripture references, I would need to alter points one and three.

By the time prayers are finished, I have rewritten almost half of my talk in my mind. Joy has become my theme, almost as if it has written itself right into the script. What surprises me is that joy is not what I had so carefully planned, but somehow it seems right.

Nevertheless, I feel at loose ends as we leave the room and proceed to the main hall. I have never rewritten my talk ten minutes before starting time before. I usually do not tell stories not already in the script or use points not previously outlined, or quote verses not rehearsed. I hope I can remember the details. I breathe a silent prayer of helplessness as I take my place behind the podium. I feel myself carried along even as I begin with my unplanned theme. Amazingly, I do not forget one detail.

"Ruth, did you plan your theme with the decoration committee? Do you realize what the banner behind you spelled?" someone rushes to the front to ask as soon as I finish my talk. I turn around and there, etched in large, gold trim are the three letters: "J-O-Y." I had been so preoccupied beforehand, I had not even noticed.

"That banner was a last minute addition," the chairman of the decorations committee tells me when I ask about it. "I grabbed it from my front hall as I walked out the door to come. When I heard your opening illustration, I knew why I'd been inspired to bring it. And to think, I had no idea you would be speaking on joy!"

I tell her the miracle of prayer time and how the talk had divinely rewritten itself. "Makes you feel you can trust

God with the details, doesn't it?" I ask her as we give each other a hug.

I leave the hall this morning, more convinced than ever that when I submit to the gentle nudges of God, I can know he is working and reworking all things together for good, even when it means rewriting the script ten minutes before I speak. I am certain God likes well-prepared talks, but should he choose to alter my plans, I trust I will remember the lesson of today and submit to his alterations.

Reunion

As I walk through these crowded corridors of humanity, I look into faces I've never seen before. All these people are going somewhere—home maybe, corporate headquarters, exotic islands, army barracks, or plush hotels. Who knows exactly where they are going, or exactly what emotions I see in their faces here on concourse D of Chicago's O'Hare Airport?

Tonight as I walk toward the SwissAir gate, only one face matters. She is waiting for me far away—a continent, an ocean, and twenty hours away. Her face is the one I have nourished and nurtured, cuddled and cared for, and studied from infancy to youth. I wonder to myself, *How has her face changed over the months since she left for school in Germany?* I know instinctively that everything will have changed and yet nothing will have changed. She is my daughter; I am her mother. When we're together, that's all that will matter.

I settle into my seat, listen to the in-flight instructions, and watch impatiently the movie screen where the red moving arrow charts our progress—Detroit, Albany, St. Lawrence Seaway, St. John's Newfoundland—such slow progress.

Crossing the Atlantic will take forever, I think to myself as I try to find a comfortable position to sleep. *And tomorrow will never come.* I close my eyes and try to remember Jori's face, her voice, her movements. *Strange how much I have forgotten in six months. Strange, also, how much I remember.* The mother-daughter bond is strong, unlike any other. Sleep comes as slowly as the miles seem to pass.

Sunrise and Switzerland! The day of our reunion! All other moments are simply to be endured—mere vehicles that carry me toward that one moment when I see Jori. I walk mechanically through the airport, see Swiss soldiers with machine guns, hear unknown languages around me, look at signs I do not understand. Smells, sight, sounds— all foreign to my senses. But nothing distracts me. I go directly to the ticket counter to buy my train pass to Romanshorn. There is but one agenda to my day.

As I watch the Swiss landscape, I count the moments and the number of stops until I reach Romanshorn. Ten more minutes and I will be with Jori. My heart beats so loudly I'm sure the woman across from me can hear it. *What will Jori look like? What will she do? What will she say?* Again and again, I picture the moment of reunion.

And suddenly it is here. Jori is running toward me, arms outstretched, bouquet of welcoming flowers in hand, tears streaming down her face. We are together and we are home, standing there by the railroad tracks in a little town in Switzerland. It is as if all our lives we have been waiting for this one moment of reunion.

As we stroll arm in arm toward the ferry that will carry us on the final lap of our journey, I think to myself, *Today I have glimpsed eternity.* I have known in part what reunion will be *That Day* when my heavenly Father welcomes me home. May I live with as much anticipation for my heavenly reunion as I have known for this earthly reunion with Jori.

CHAPTER THREE

Secrets of Sacrificing

The Way to Good-byes

I've walked this concourse so many times,
It is the way to good-byes
Every time
I ache all the way to the gate.

You are going away again
To places I have not seen
And cannot predict.
What waits for you out there beyond the blue?
I do not know.
How will you be different when you come back?
I do not know that either.
It is scary
This business of letting you go
It pulls against everything my mother-heart wants to do
   Protect
   Possess
   Preside over
But I stand here at this gate today
And once again watch as the giant bird lifts you into the sky
Carrying you away.

As I wipe my tears,
His words come ever so gently,
"I loved her before you did.
Now trust her to me."

I walk away from the gate
Take a deep breath
And say with every ounce of courage I can muster,
"Okay, Lord,
I return her to you."

Once again
I have known the bittersweet of letting go.

Lights Don't Sparkle in Pakistan

What is success? I ask myself this morning as I sadly
fold the paper after reading of yet another fallen hero
exposed. Toppled from his popularity pedestal, he was not
who everyone thought he was. All the world was fooled
and now shocked.

By normal standards, he had been successful, produc-
tive, knowledgeable, and articulate. His contemporaries
had respected him. He had glittered under the lights, but
corroded beneath the pressure. *What happened to him?* I
wonder.

Still thinking about integrity, I park my car next to
the space for the handicapped outside the missions
headquarters. I have come here on a quick errand for my
daughter, who leaves in three days for a work project in

Aruba. Following directions on the wall to the purchasing department, I walk down the stairs, straight ahead, and to the left. I enter a small room, sparsely furnished with a few metal shelves full of miscellaneous staples for overseas workers: vitamins, first-aid supplies, toothbrushes, packaged food, note cards, books on mission history and mission strategy. On the window ledge that looks out on ground level, there is an African violet, wood carvings from South America, porcelain from the Orient, and brass from India. I sense the world around me as I stand here in this two-by-four cubicle and ask for light bulbs, computer disks, and a year's supply of vitamins for the missionaries in Aruba.

As I turn my attention to the woman filling my order, I notice the lines on her face—lines of wisdom, contentment, a steady spirit. I don't know this woman, and I don't know one detail of her life, yet I can tell her life hasn't been cluttered with sparkle and glitter. She has worked hard and has known simplicity and joy.

As she takes my order and meticulously writes the numbers—order number, purchase number, missionary's account number, I notice the age spots on her hands. We go through a swinging door and look for more numbers written on brown shipping packages, stacked on more metal shelves. She searches for my package of light bulbs, vitamins, and computer disks as though she is completing an order for the president of the United States. I sense her greatness and wonder *What makes her great?* And I think again of the fallen hero.

As we are going back through the swinging door, I ask her to tell me about herself. She shares that she is a missionary nurse, who served a lifetime in the remote mountains of Pakistan, lived through two Indian wars, and then retired to the States to serve some more. *What makes her great?* I answer my own question. She has lived with integrity.

The television cameras didn't find her in Pakistan. No one ever wrote a book about this quiet servant, living out her days in the backside of civilization. Now she writes and reads numbers in a basement stockroom with a gracious contentment born out of years of honest, joyful service to others.

Today I have seen success firsthand, success as God meant it to be. I have met integrity and I am filled with hope for myself, my children, and my world.

On Security, Sacrifice, and Greyhound Buses

L ove isn't love until it goes out of its way for another." I've made that statement often, but never have I thought about sacrifice the way I do today.

As I come through the door of my Sunday school class, I hear "Ruth Senter, wait up." I see a college friend, one with whom I share unforgettable memories of a ten-week trip to Europe, where we toured Britain and the Continent with a women's choral group. Our paths had crossed occasionally over the years, but today some twenty-five years later, those memories come alive again.

"I just wanted to tell you that I've never forgotten that, out of almost sixty women in our group, your father was the only father who came to Montreal to see us off when we sailed for England. I can still see your dad standing there on the dock alone, waving good-bye with his white handkerchief while we sang, 'God Be with You Til We Meet Again.'"

I remembered, too. The scene was forever etched on my memory, so were our circumstances then. Dad was a part-time volunteer pastor. Money could not have been more scarce. He was cutting meat at a grocery store to put bread on the table for his family of seven. There was no money or time for such luxuries as a five-hundred-mile trip to Montreal just to watch your daughter's ship sail for England. Every piece of meat cut meant another bill paid, another meal on the table.

But there he was at the ship terminals on the morning of our departure. I had seen him coming through the crowd with his wide, welcoming smile. His topcoat was wrinkled, his eyes red from his overnight ride on a Greyhound bus, but I knew he was thrilled to be there.

I don't remember ever having felt so loved. I knew as soon as our ship sailed, he would return to the bus station for another eight hour ride home. Nothing more—no shopping spree in the city, no sightseeing, not even dinner out at a nice hotel. He had come for his daughter, even when he couldn't afford it.

Other dads could have come by plane and stayed at the nearest Holiday Inn for the night. But the dad who could probably afford it the least gave the most.

My platitudes on sacrifice come so easily, I think to myself. I give when it is convenient—when the bills have been paid, when my schedule has free time. And I wonder *Is it love?*

True love—the going-out-of-one's-way kind of love, leaves no doubt in the mind of the loved one. *My dad did that for me!* No wonder, that today, twenty-five years later, I am still secure in my earthly father's love *and* in the love of my heavenly Father.

Esther

Standing in my mother's dining room, I cry as I read a letter written on delicate parchment with Oriental flowers across the top and Japanese characters running down the side.

> She was one of the most gentle, loving women we have known. She took us in when we were almost complete strangers. We will miss her warm smile and gracious hugs.

I cry with the Japanese scientist who wrote the letter. Although he is far away in Japan, we are together in our grief. I cry with Pastor John, who now stands on the other side of the dining room table. He is delivering a Christmas gift to us, but no doubt he needs to reminisce with those who knew and loved his wife, so recently taken from him. I cry tears of grief.

For a while, I am not a forty-two-year-old mother of two, standing in my mother's dining room on Christmas vacation. I remember being fifteen again and sitting in the back room of a deserted skating rink, turned into a church. There were only eight of us gathered around the circle that Sunday morning. We were certain that we were the most alert, most responsive Sunday school students a teacher could ever have. Esther told us so, and we never doubted our teacher's judgment. Esther had a way of making us feel comfortable with who we were, even though we were struggling through that self-conscious, awkward age of fifteen. She valued us as rare treasures. She fed us Sunday dinners, took us picnicking in the park, invited us to her cottage at the lake. We were her friends and she treated us with the dignity and delight due a friend. She was our teacher in more ways than one.

Today, I hold the parchment tribute in my hand and reminisce about Esther. She taught us God's Word, and so much more. As a result of knowing her, we were more satisfied with who we were. She gave us love in its purest form. Now I stand with her husband and grieve her absence. I also pray there will be more high-school Sunday school teachers like her.

Giving 'Til It Hurts

Sometimes I am willing to give when the giving is easy—when I give something that doesn't mean much to me anyway. Seldom have I been so reminded of it as I am tonight, as I sit here in church and see my son's picture flashed on a giant screen in the front of the sanctuary. As the slide projector clicks through its carousel, we watch the weeks and the mission work project unfold. Nick and his high-school friends have dug trenches for water pipes, built a shed for the missionaries, taught vacation Bible school, and been pals and buddies to the Navajo children who flocked to the church programs.

The rewards of sacrifice, of giving, I think to myself as I view high schoolers on top of tin roofs, knee-deep in mud and waist-high in ditches. High schoolers pounding nails, swinging axes, hoisting beams, and playing with children. High schoolers holding a wordless book that tells the story of Jesus' love. High schoolers playing ball and nursing sore muscles. The gifts of love are plainly visible. I am impressed by our youth who gave so committedly. But I am rebuked by the slide of Nick that flashes on the screen. It is the last day of vacation Bible school. Nick and his friends are handing out T-shirts, which our church sent for the Navajo children. "There were just enough shirts for everyone," the narrator said, "except for Hermon. We ran out of shirts just as we got to him."

Click went the slide projector and there stood Nick without a shirt. His arm was around Hermon who was wearing a red "Crusader Basketball Camp" T-shirt. I recognized it as Nick's prize for winning the free-throw contest at basketball camp just the week before he left for his mission trip. The red shirts were reserved for the winners, and I knew how much Nick treasured his. The narrator continued, "So Nick took off his own shirt and gave it to Hermon and rode the forty-five minutes back to camp without a shirt."

I cried quiet tears of motherly love, tears of gratitude for Nick's lessons of sacrificial love, and tears of repentance for me. *Forgive me, Lord, for giving so easily when there's really no great loss for me. Teach me to give even when it hurts.*

When Social Security Speaks

I'm sorry, Ms. Senter. We cannot issue you a new driver's license without verification of your social security number." For the third time I patiently try to explain that I don't have a social security card anymore. It was stolen at the train station along with my driver's license, wallet, credit cards, bank cards, cash, and children's pictures.

Isn't it bad enough that I have to be here today, fighting traffic, facing long, irritating lines of people who would rather be anywhere but here? I take a number and wait my turn, only to be told, "The computers are down at this facility today, but you may obtain a license at another Secretary of State's office, ten miles east, right off the 290 Expressway." And all for crimes I didn't commit. I am still chafing at the thought that some stranger, pushing through post-Christmas rush at Union Station would have the nerve to zip open my purse and steal my wallet. The inconvenience of it all has not been made any easier today when I arrive here, only to find that I have to keep driving—first to a town thirty minutes away to obtain a social security clearance, and then another half hour to a second facility where, hopefully, the computers are functioning.

As though I have nothing better to do with my time, I mutter to myself as I take a number and join a third line, this one at the social security office. I sense that this is not a happy place to be. Toddlers whine. Adults complain. Being reduced to a number seems to have drained those of us who wait of any semblance of goodwill and peaceful understanding.

"Never have I seen such a rude place in all my life," an old man with a leathery face laments as he pounds his cane on the tile floor. "Have to take a number before they will even answer your question." He addresses his comments to no one in particular, but we all nod in silent accord. The impersonalization of it all does not sit well with me either, especially when I know there is more to come after I leave this place.

And all because someone had the nerve to steal my wallet. I return to the source of my misery and feel my jaw tighten again. I have gone through the scenario before. An unguarded moment. Divided attention. Rushing crowd around me. And how often have I reminded my teenage daughter to carry her purse in front of her when she's in a crowd. I do not easily forgive myself or the thief.

I am still bothered and disturbed, not only by the theft, but by the hassles of the day, when my number is called and I step to the counter. I am aware that someone in a pink coat steps up beside me. I am also aware that it is not her turn. *I sat and waited. Let her do the same*, I think to myself.

"I'm sorry miss, you'll have to take a number and wait your turn." The clerk speaks the irritation I feel.

"But all I needed to know was. . . ." Two small children pull at her coat, and the baby in her arms cries a hacking cry. The clerk repeats her instructions with growing force and irritation.

"Please, ma'am," the young mother starts again. This time her words come out with a sob. "All I wanted to know . . . is this where I get the certificate for my husband's death?"

We are stopped short, the clerk and I. Neither of us knows what to say. I want to gather the mother into my arms, wipe her tears, hold her crying baby, calm her restless toddlers. Instead I step back from the counter and mumble something about being sorry and, "Go ahead." Trite words next to a certificate for a husband's death.

The clerk hands me the necessary forms, and I return to my seat to write. But I have been silenced and humbled. *A lost wallet, and she has lost a husband,* I reflect as I fill out the forms. My losses seemed tragic until now.

I drive to my next stop with a thankful heart. In my mind, I see the woman in the pink coat again and hear her sob. And even as I drive, I pray about her loss and begin the process of forgetting about my own.

PART II: FINDING GOD THROUGH UNEXPECTED PLACES

CHAPTER FOUR

Secrets of Being
Caught Unaware
"The Road"

I follow a road
That winds among
The dead, lifeless forms of
Trees
Like skeletons with no flesh
Bones with no meat
Endless rows of monotone
Dull
Drab
Gray.
I go on
Through the gray
I cannot go back
For the road points ahead
And
Eventually
It
Turns the corner
Into
Remnants of fall
Iridescent reds
Oranges
Gold that shimmers
Like some garment of nobility.

Endless colors of autumn
Surround me
Endless skeletons of winter
Behind me
And who knows what
Ahead.
It is a mix of seasons
This road I'm on
Life is a mix of seasons
Of
Golden fall
And
Winter gray
But I must go on
For
The Road points ahead.

Miracle in Federal Express

Federal Express trucks don't often bring with them re-minders in faith, but today the Federal Express truck that pulls into my driveway does.

As far as I'm concerned, Federal Express trucks don't generally do home deliveries. In fact, I don't ever remember seeing one in my driveway or in any of the driveways of my neighborhood. To me, Federal Express is part of the trapping of high-pressure corporations where every second counts and yesterday's mail has to be rushed through the night to arrive before breakfast the next day. Certainly not a usual accoutrement of daily living for the suburban housewife.

So foreign is the notion of Federal Express that when the editor on the phone gives me the Federal Express number and asks me to please use it to send her the copy she needs by tomorrow morning, I can't even remember having seen a Federal Express box in our town.

"Oh, I'm sure there is one closer than you think," she answers casually. I am a bit bothered by the hassle of it all. I've never used Federal Express. I don't know the procedure. Don't have the proper envelopes. Don't have time to go snooping around the town looking for a blue and orange box. Besides my day is already planned and my schedule doesn't include Federal Express.

I am already feeling the pressure as I hang up the phone, pull out the yellow pages and go about scanning the endless columns of black ink. I mutter as I scan.

. . . *Post office is three minutes away and who knows where Federal Express has hidden their boxes. Who knows where they've hidden their ads here in this yellow maze in the rear of my phone book. Postal Service? Express Mail? Mailing? Do I look under P or E or M?*

I am still sputtering and muttering when the doorbell rings. I open the door and there in my driveway is a blue and white Federal Express truck!

"What are you doing here!" I blurt out to the man in brown.

As far as he knows, he is simply there delivering an overnight letter to a graduate student who lives in our basement. I explain my dilemma. He gives me the proper forms, an envelope and points me to the Federal Express box two blocks from my front door.

He leaves as quickly as he has come. I close the door and stand silent in the front hall. My muttering and sputtering has ceased. The man in brown is a gentle reminder that God sometimes disrupts my flow and shows up in ways he's never shown up before.

Why? I don't know exactly why. Perhaps just to stop my muttering. Perhaps to slow me down. Perhaps just to remind me that he is God—Lord of the universe and yes, even Lord of the Federal Express.

Ways of the Wilderness

When I was young we sang a song that went like this: "My Lord knows the way through the wilderness. All I have to do is follow." I think of that song tonight as we sit in the dark, surrounded by a wilderness of sorts.

During the day, Michigan State Highway 35, which follows the shoreline north of Green Bay, is a nature-lover's paradise. By night, it is a long, deserted patch of darkness. Certain we will not miss much, the children and I settle down to sleep and leave the cares of the road to Daddy.

Suddenly, monotony comes to a screeching halt as the massive hulk of a deer slams against headlights, grill, radiator, and fan belt. The van shudders on impact, smoke hisses, the motor groans, and the buck lies dead in the ditch. We sit immobilized. In their tenderness, the children think immediately of Bambi, while Daddy remembers that it has been at least thirty minutes since he's seen lights.

As we look through the door, we spot a lighted sign, "Parcells' Bayside Park Resort, Restaurant and Motel." Later, sitting around a table of food and knowing that we have a warm, comfortable room for the night and an offer from Mr. Parcell to help us get to town in the morning, I think again of the words to the song. I reaffirm the principle I learned as a child. God doesn't spare us from the wilderness, but he does know the way through, even down to the location of Parcell's Bayside Park Resort.

"And we have only been open a week," Mr. Parcell's eyes sparkle. "You are our very first customer." When we stood to leave, he does not allow us to pay for our dinners. "On the house," is all he says.

We walk through the crisp fall night toward our motel room. I stop to listen to the waves lap the shoreline. I look up into the night-time sky. How like my heavenly Father to make even the wilderness a reminder of his love.

Picture, Picture on the Wall

I remember when Jesus was a person to me—with skin on. I looked at his kind face smiling from my Sunday school take-home paper, and in typical four-year-old-fashion, I said to my Sunday school teacher, "I love Jesus."

Then I was a child. Now I am an adult with teenage children of my own. I have traded in my Sunday school pictures of Jesus' healing a leper, gathering little children into his arms, bringing a dead girl back to life. My images of God are much more sophisticated and conceptualized; my theology, more abstract. As an adult, I love God intellectually and verbally. I have moved beyond the need for pictures.

Or have I? This morning as I wait for my laundry, I study the pictures advertising this local dry cleaners—men in water-repellent trench coats, brides in moth-proofed wedding gowns, women in wrinkle-free white linen suits.

But there in the corner, behind the cash register, another picture catches my eye.

When I was growing up, this picture hung above my daddy's desk, where he prepared his sermons and had his quiet time. Probably this picture had more to do with my faith than any theology book I ever studied. As a child I memorized every detail. Christ, arrayed in white, stood outside knocking at an arched stone door with a tiny window at the top. He looked as though he would wait all night if he needed to for the person inside to open the door. Even as a child, I was awed by the fact that the door had no outside handle. "I love Jesus," I would say to my daddy as I stood and looked at the gentle man outside the door.

As I continue to wait for my laundry and study this picture, I go through the mental gymnastics of trying to figure out whether the door really did have a handle or not. *If God already knows, do I really have a choice?* I ask myself. This morning, however, I am not moved by mental gymnastics. I am moved by love—pure love that does not force itself on anyone, love that waits, for a day, a year, maybe even a lifetime for someone to open a door. God always gives choices. It is what salvation is all about—my choice to open the door and invite him in.

I wonder how many other pictures from childhood are stored in my memory, pictures that, if I move beyond my abstract sophistication, could remind me of God's love and help me to apply my faith. Who says when I become adult I don't need concrete reminders of who God is and what he is like? Maybe I need them even more.

Jeremiah Was a Bullfrog

'T is the season for joy. I see it written in the air, on the rooftop of the college men's dorm just down the street. I hear it blown through a trumpet on the street corner as shoppers rush home with their treasures—"Joy to the World." I hang it on my Christmas tree in wooden letters blocked over a green wreath with a red bow attached. Now I stop by the coffee shop for my morning cup of coffee. I hear joy here, too, but joy of a different kind—blasted over some local soft-rock station.

> *Jeremiah was a bullfrog.*
> *Was a good friend of mine.*
> *Never understood a single word he said,*
> *But I help him drink his wine*
>
> *Singing*
> *Joy to the world*
> *All the boys and girls now*

> Joy to the fishes in the deep blue sea,
> Joy to you and me.

I am struck by the irony of joy—on a roof, on a street corner, on a Christmas tree, and in the rhythm for a catchy beat. Joy is manufactured to maintain the holiday mood.

I wonder, as I move through the season, what happens if joy never gets further than rooftops, street corners, Christmas trees, or trite, pop songs.

I lie in bed and stare into the dark. Sleep does not come. Only two more days until my family arrives from all corners of the East. The house is not clean, cookies are not baked, gifts are not wrapped, cards are not sent. The ice and snow slows movement outside; swollen glands, a feverish brow, and a congested head slows movement inside. In fact, my movement has come to a halt. *I don't have time for this,* I moan to myself as the hours tick away and holiday preparations remain undone. *Where is joy now?* I ask myself.

Five A.M., and the phone rings—family emergency six hours south. Mark jumps in the car and leaves. *Another day wiped out and just when I needed him,* I sigh. The calendar says December 23. I fold my "Today's list of things to do" and stick it into the drawer. "The best laid plans"—I am already two weeks behind. And I wonder, *Where is joy now?*

The family has gathered. It has been three years since we've grouped in this exact way. The hours are precious. I hang on to every minute.

Then on Christmas Eve, the long-distance phone call comes, disrupting the flow. "Grandpa has to fly home to Pennsylvania," I say to Nick as he comes into the house later on in the evening. "One of his parishioners died, and the family wants him for the funeral, but at least he will be here Christmas day." I try not to sound disappointed. And I wonder as brother Denny and I drive Grandpa to the airport, two days ahead of schedule, *Where is joy now?*

The post-Christmas crowd tonight seems especially frantic to board the *Broadway Limited* for New York City. Mother and I push our way through the gate and along the platform. Mark moves far ahead with the luggage. I feel the tug at my purse. *Only the press of bodies*, I think at first. I look down. *I am sure this purse was zipped a minute ago.* I stare into an empty purse.

"Wallet, forty dollars in cash, driver's license, credit cards, social security card, cherished pictures of my kids, bank cards. . . ." I go down the list for the police officer who mechanically copies it from behind a gray steel desk and piles of cluttered miscellanea.

"Happens all the time," he says as he completes his scribbles. "Can't promise much hope for ever seeing your wallet again. These people are pros. Probably blocks from here by now."

But just in case, I look in every garbage can in Union Station, then Mark and I head back into Chicago's post-Christmas night. And I wonder, as moisture gathers in the corners of my eyes at the thought of lost treasures, *Where is joy now?*

"Joy to the world."

I think as we drive toward home that joy can stay on the rooftops and street corners and Christmas trees. Or, it can move inside me. The choice is mine.

I conclude, *If joy doesn't move inside, it really isn't joy at all. For the fruit of the Spirit is . . . joy. And joy is a condition of my spirit, not a condition of my surroundings.* I think of it now, even as I reach out in the dark and feel an empty purse.

When Small Things Matter

The dark spot on the trunk lid of my white Pontiac seemed innocent enough at first. Small, barely noticeable. You could almost pass it off as dust. Why bother about dust? A quick drive through the car wash every now and then plus semi-annual wax jobs seemed maintenance enough for dusty, dark spots and whatever else accumulated on the surface of a car from week to week. Besides, I'm not one to spend time on trivialities, especially when they're barely noticeable.

"Looks like some rust coming through the lid of your trunk," Mark said to me one day as he walked past the back of my car. "Maybe you should get Mike to take a look at it."

Mike owned the auto body shop down the road and was an expert on car exteriors. He'd dealt with our automotive crises before—reconstructing our van after we'd hit a deer in Michigan and piecing together my yellow Pontiac LeMans after a Northern Illinois gas truck and I arrived at the corner of Scott and Prairie Streets at precisely the same time.

I don't think this is a problem for Mike, I thought to myself. *Not big enough. Why worry him about the small stuff.*

And so I ignored the rust spot and spent time instead scurrying for the nearest car wash whenever white turned to gray or the shine became dull. I was much more concerned with the overall look of my car than with the speck of rust that was slowly and inconspicuously eating away the lid of my trunk. But one day I noticed the speck of rust was no longer a speck. Overnight it seemed, it had grown to the size of half a dollar. Sure enough, now it was noticeable. Any car following me could spot the rust, I was sure. The cancer had shown up on the outside. Now was the time for action.

I found an old tube of automobile touch-up paint Mike had once given me for repairing minor nicks and chips. "Apply liberally to damaged area" the label read. And I did. I piled on layers of globby white, smoothed over the edges with sandpaper and smiled with satisfaction that my rust problem had been so easily dealt with.

But there are no permanent cover-up jobs for rust. Before many days had passed, I noticed the ominous black spot again. This time its shape resembled a giant squid with tentacles reaching in all directions. I stared at the strange blackish-orange corrosion and thought with dismay of rain and snow pouring through the rust hole into my trunk. Rust was not just a cosmetic problem. Now it was a practical problem.

"What do you think?" I asked Mike the next day when I stopped at the body shop for an opinion. Mike studied my trunk lid long and hard. He felt the rust, took sand paper to its surface, poked at it from underneath.

"Too late," he mumbled under his breath. "It's already spread to the seam. When the seam's affected, the whole trunk is damaged. Only a hundred ninety five bucks and I'll give you a new trunk." He smiled at me, but I sensed he understood the progression of neglect for "little" things.

Today as I write a check to Mike for repairs on a damaged trunk, I am reminded of the subtleties of sin. Small omissions. Tiny lapses. Unnoticeable inconsistencies. Secret disloyalties. And sin, when not repaired in the beginning, brings damage, sometimes irreparable damage. It took a rust spot in the lid of my car trunk to remind me.

CHAPTER FIVE

Secrets of Solitude

"The Lighthouse"

You stand there
Single
Solitary
Unmoveable in the storm
Your outline
Blurred by fog
Butted by waves
Bathed in monotone gray.

Sea
Sky
Lighthouse
All are one
Except for the beacon at the top
Which blinks red
And turns ships instinctively
Toward port
Like a comforting Holy Spirit
Illuminating
Guiding
Guarding the Harbor
Bringing me safely
Through.

The Bag That Was Left Behind

I am ten minutes down the road before I remember my bag—the one I always carry, stocked with *National Geographic, Country Living,* my writing pad, and the blue needlepoint I have been working on for four years. I have a forty-five-minute train ride to the city and nothing to do. I feel the waste of time. In this day and time, I do not throw chunks of forty-five minutes away with nothing to show for it in the end. But I have no choice. I am already running late, and there is no time to go back for my bag.

Once on the train, I search in vain for a newspaper. I can't even catch up on the world, and no one is selling coffee in the aisles. The scenery is not bad this morning with the sun shining on the snow, and for a while that satisfies me. But I am restless, as if I am forgetting something or letting someone down. Suddenly the truth dawns: I have lost the ability to sit and do nothing. Somehow I have been conditioned to feel that to sit with nothing to do is a waste of time. I am acting as though I believe I'm wasting time, but I don't really believe that, or do I?

I try to remember the last time I simply sat without my Bible, a devotional book, a novel, needlepoint, a pen in my hand, or listening to the radio or a tape, without someone's talking to me. I'm amazed I cannot remember when. I am always doing something. I begin to think about people in the Bible who knew how to sit and do nothing. Israel had just suffered two humiliating defeats at the hands of the Benjamites, who were at war. They could not afford to sit and do nothing. But by the third day of battle, when forces seemed about to destroy them, someone led the Israelites back to Bethel and their altar, where "they sat weeping before the LORD . . . they fasted that day until evening. . . ." (Judg. 20:26). The next day, God gave them victory.

I think of David, who had just been promised the kingdom. The prophet Nathan had delivered the message. It seems to me as if it would have been time for David to shift into high gear and organize his reign. But the first thing he did was to go and "sit before the LORD" (2 Sam. 7:18). And when David did speak, he had something to say.

I hear the conductor call out "Oak Park. All out for Oak Park." I hear the sounds around me, but I also hear God's gentle reminder, "Be still and know that I am God." (Ps. 46:10). How fortunate that I forgot my bag.

Lost Paradise

Once in a while life has a way of jarring my illusions, I remind myself today as I take my daily walk along Salt Creek and around the park district lagoon. I was created for quiet places like these, where water laps gently at the shoreline, fall geese soar overhead in perfect Florida-bound formation, and cottonwoods whisper secrets to each other. Today I drink deeply of the world as it was meant to be.

The fall evening is mellow, and I am mellow with it. We both have laid aside the briskness of the day. It is time for closing in, shutting down, putting to sleep realities of the day—schedules, obligations, duties, the everlasting tick of the clock that reminds me of so much to do. Here in this peaceful spot where illusions can take wing, I imagine the world as it was created to be. There are no harsh words spoken in haste, no Ds on algebra quizzes, no slamming doors that close off communication for a while, no tugs-of-war—my priorities versus yours.

For a moment there is peace. I stop to sit on the park bench and watch the day depart. It slips over the edge of the water effortlessly. But then, all of nature here in this isolated Eden seems to move smoothly—no human genius to foul up the order of things.

I listen to the sounds of wholeness—geese honking, water lapping, trees whispering, crickets beginning their nocturnal tune-up. Oh, that life could be less noisy, that I could sit forever in quiet places listening to God's voice. Oh, that life would tune out the trash and send its messages on pure air waves.

But my illusions are not to be. Two boys, somewhere between the ages eight and twelve, are fishing, first in apparent harmony, now in frustrated anger over tangled fishing lines. The air is alive with their four-letter words screeching across the peaceful water to where I am sitting. Suddenly, there is no reason for me to stay here. The spell is broken. I stand and move hastily down the path. This is not Eden. I smile to myself at my feeble attempts to make it so. This is the world bent out of shape—the world I must live in for a while.

I am only three blocks from home, but in many ways, I am a long way from home. Today I understand anew what the writer of Hebrews meant when he said, "We are aliens and strangers on earth" (Heb. 11:13). No matter how hard I try, I cannot recreate Eden prematurely. But then, maybe that is what hope is all about. I live in the midst of fallenness, but I live with one foot squarely in Eden—with a longing for home, which fills each day with hope.

Invader in My Kitchen

I am not particularly looking for a lesson on marriage
at one o'clock in the morning, but sometimes life's best
learning comes when I'm not looking for it.

The night is peaceful as I slide into my down-filled
sleeping bag. Nocturnal voices of the woods lull me into
restfulness: wind rustling through the pines, crickets
humming, frogs ker-plunking down by the water's edge,
and a whippoorwill's calling. *Simple pleasures of life in the
wild*, I think as I drift into oblivion.

I awaken with a start. I hear strange sounds coming
from the vicinity of our picnic table, just beyond our tent.
Someone or something is rattling pans. I can tell by a
flashlight glance at sleeping forms around me that it is not
one of us. As the rattling grows louder, I shake Mark.

"Honey, something is out there. Quick. Go chase it
away."

Always ready to provide back-up support so Mark can handle the sudden crisis, I shine the flashlight toward the entrance of the tent. Meanwhile, Mark, in his usual calm, thoughtful manner, is slowly crawling out of his warm cocoon. When the rattling continues, I am imagining the worst. "Hurry, please."

But my brave adventurer is in no hurry. "I'm not going to chase anything until I see what it is." He stands motionless behind the zipped-up tent opening and shines the flashlight into the clearing where the picnic table stands. Now I hear a thud and pans falling. "Honey, aren't you going to do something?"

He doesn't answer. As is often the case, I am bothered that Mark is not moving faster, the way I would. Finally, he turns.

"Relax, he's gone. Biggest skunk I've ever seen. Just stood there and looked at me, then waddled off. Can you imagine what would have happened had I gone charging out of here and startled him?"

He doesn't need to elaborate. My imagination can fill in the details. As I drift back to sleep, I smile through the darkness. *Thank you, Lord, that Mark and I are not alike. And thank you that he doesn't just go charging in as I would have done.*

The next time I am frustrated because I don't think my husband is moving fast enough, I hope I will remember the lesson of the skunk who visited my kitchen in the wild—the lesson that sometimes differences, as irritating as they may be, can really be our salvation.

Good Things Come Easy?

Our world has been sold a bill of goods. I am reminded of it this morning when I stop at the nearby 7 Eleven for a morning cup of coffee. Written in bold declaration across the middle of my styrofoam cup is the message: "7 Eleven. Where Good Things Come Easy."

I chuckle to myself that some slick advertising agency knew that I, in all my humanness, want good things to come easy. How clever of them to choose this slogan for 7 Eleven quick-stop grocery stores.

How like the world to go to great lengths to convince me that I can have all the good things in life without effort if only I shop the right places, wear the right perfume, cruise to the right vacation spots.

But there really is nothing new under the sun, I muse. Satan has been offering this deception since the Fall. It all started with his offer to Eve, If you eat this fruit, you will be wise, you will be like God—easy short-cut route to God-likeness.

The deception continues today. For every Christian value, the world offers its cheap, easy imitation. The fruit of the Spirit is love, joy, peace. But the world offers romance, happiness, the good life, and ease with a cup of coffee from 7 Eleven. Right environment produces fulfillment, the world seems to say to me.

If I am not careful, I fall for those lines. I work to make my environment right; I manufacture my own counterfeit "fruit," then hang it on my life like I hang ornaments on my Christmas tree. This fruit is seasonal, temporary, external. It does not come from my heart anymore than my white porcelain ornaments grow from my Christmas tree. My artificial fruit comes with the holiday season, and when the season ends, so does the produce— the love, joy, peace.

The "fruit of the Spirit" is not seasonal, not a condition of my world, but a condition of my heart. It comes from the Life within me, not the life around me. Genuine fruit is a process, not a quick "fix" at the corner grocery store. It comes hard, not easily, and grows through tears (Ps. 126:5), not through short-cuts and rose gardens.

If then, there is to be genuine fruit in my life, I must cultivate the Life within. I must remain at home with God (John 15), read his Word, think his thoughts, keep conversation with him, study his ways. Easy assignment? Definitely not. Good fruit? Unmistakably yes.

What then do I do with coffee cups that promise "good things come easy?" I sip my coffee, enjoy its flavor, and then sadly deposit my cup in the garbage. I am sad because of a system where coffee cups sell a philosophy of life. Sad, too, for all the people, Christians included, who buy into easy, short-cut commitments.

PART III: FINDING GOD THROUGH EMOTIONS

CHAPTER SIX

Secrets of Belonging

"Welcome Home"

"Welcome Home."
Joyful words
Spoken on a cold winter's night
We have been absent from each other
Expanded distance between us
Miles and miles of silent space.
I was not made for distance
Nor for silent space.

I return
You are there
Arms open
Eyes expectant
I am home
And
I am welcome
It is "The Father's" touch.

Love at Home

I have often come home to this big white house on the hill, with its rambling front porch and its spreading maples. Just as often, I have driven down its circular driveway, waved good-bye to my parents, and headed first toward college, then toward marriage, ministry, children, and life in the Midwest. But never before have I realized as I do tonight how much I have taken with me from this place.

It has been an exhausting two days. I drove several hundred miles on the first day to keep a speaking engagement, lectured from ten in the morning until ten at night on the second day, met old friends, greeted new ones, reminisced about the good old days with relatives I had not seen for years.

During these last two days, I looked into eyes that have known suffering, held hands that have touched pain, hugged to my heart people whose love has grown cold. These have been days when I have given and given and given again—days that would have been exhausting, except for the receiving. From the moment I stepped off the plane and found myself enfolded in my father's arms, I received. All the way home in the car as he asked about the details of my life—about Mark, about Jori and Nick, about my work— my father cared about every intricacy of my life. I could get away with long elaborate details and know he would listen like no one else would. I rode home secure in his love.

Then I received again as I climbed the stairs to the porch, opened the front door, smelled the aroma of homemade soup and freshly baked bread. Mother was there waiting for me with the love that only a mother for forty-four years could possibly give. To her, I was her little girl come home; to me, it was all that mattered. Forget the lectures and books and business that brought me to them. I was here to receive, to drink deeply of their love.

Tonight, some forty-eight hours later, as I look down from the plane on the lights of the city I've called home for the past twenty-seven years, I think back to the home I've just left. There is a unique beauty in that old home, from Grandpa Martin's grandfather's clock, which chimes in the corner of the living room, to the old Tiffany lamp, which hangs over the dining room table, and the maple blanket chest that Great-grandpa Zimmerman made for my grandma as a gift on her wedding day.

But tonight, it's not the beauty of that home I have just left that sustains me, that carries me home on wings rather than in pieces. I step from the plane and I am invigorated and renewed, even after a grueling non-stop two days. I return with freshness.

And I think, as I walk the concourse toward my

waiting car that what I bring back with me from my parents and the big, old white house on the hill is the invigorating security of knowing I am loved. I remember the words of a song I heard often as a child, "There is beauty all around when there's love at home. There is joy in every sound, when there's love at home." For it is from home we gather strength to meet the world. From home we gather love to give the world. Yes, I have been home. And I have been renewed.

Put a Light in the Window

 There are more lights than usual in the windows this year," I say to Mark as we drive down our street several weeks before Christmas. "You can tell the energy crunch is over. People don't mind the electric bills anymore. Or, maybe they just feel more festive this year."

I have no idea why there are more lights in the windows of the homes along our street this year, but the lights remind me of another light. Years ago the lamp shown from the wide picture window that faced north into the woodsy pines of southern Alabama. Mother always had the white lamp with the pink rose on its base just inside the window. As a child, coming home from school on the long bus ride through winter's dusk, I could spot the lamp from half a mile down the road. I knew mother was expecting my brothers and me. Yes, eager for us. She would have the chocolate chip cookies and milk ready when we stepped inside the door.

The lamp shown on, all through my teenage years. The night would be late, but the light would shine from the window to welcome me home from a date or from a long Friday night at Brubaker's Dry Cleaning, where I worked. Mother is expecting me. Yes, eager for me. Here is a place I am warmed and welcomed. The lamp said it all.

Years have passed and the white lamp with the pink rose on its base has long since been replaced. But another lamp glows from the front living room window in the Pennsylvania home where Mother and Daddy wait for the arrival of their hungry, weary children from Illinois. I see the light from the foot of the hill. Eight hundred miles and we are home. They are expecting us, yes eager for us. The lamp is shining, and we are enfolded in love and warmth.

But I wonder today about the white candles that glow from the windows of our own house. I have put them there because I like white lights shining from windows at Christmastime. I have rushed headlong into the season of lights, stringing tiny bulbs, hauling in the pine branches, twisting cranberry colored ribbons into bows.

White porcelain ornaments gleam from the Christmas tree and Grandpa's old black barn lantern on the deacon's bench is surrounded by pine cones and greens on the front porch. Yes, the lights are on. The candles glow. The house is ready.

But I wonder. Should the Galilee Stranger walk down Arapahoe Trail, round the bend in the street, and look ahead to white lights in the windows, would he say, "they are expecting me, yes, eager for me." Or, would he walk the cold streets and look at all the glowing lights, but feel no welcome? Would he see the star, shining from the village hall, but find the baby banned from public places?

Would he hear the celebration and know he had not been invited in because the house is too full of presents, aunts, uncles, cousins, and stuffed turkey with all the trimmings?

Tonight white lights glow from our Christmas windows. *Lord, may they be to welcome you home.* "Even so come, Lord Jesus."

The Couch

It didn't seem like a big deal at the time. We redecorated the family room, got rid of the old gold couch, then when we could afford it, would buy a new one. *No one will miss a couch for a while*, I told myself. *Kids like to sit on the floor anyhow; all they really need are a few throw pillows.* Over the past year without a couch in the family room, I noticed a strange thing happening: people stopped using that room. There was no place to be close to each other. Oh, every now and then when someone needed to use the World Book Encyclopedias, he'd sit at Grandpa Hollinger's old desk and do his homework. Or, if the men in our house wanted to watch ABC's Wide World of Sports, they'd grab a pillow and sprawl on the floor. Bodies plopped down on individual chairs. But no one sat there very often and talked to each other. After dinner, everyone split for their rooms. I had a growing uneasiness that we were all going our own way without each other.

Last week we moved a new couch into the family room. It fits perfectly along the south wall, provides a focal point for the room, and says, "Stop here. Rest a while." An antique pine blanket chest from the turn of the century sits in front of it, perfect for feet, magazines, and a giant bowl of popcorn, fresh from the popper.

Now, something strange is happening again in the family room. Friday night Jori and her girlfriend sat on the couch and talked for two hours and never once went up to Jori's room. One evening I caught Nick, snuggled up on the couch next to his daddy watching a basketball game. Last night after dinner, Mark sat down beside me as I read the evening paper. We sat there together for a while, arm touching arm, like we did when we used to date. This morning when Nick needed some help with his homework he said, "Come, Mom, let's sit on the couch." He plopped down close beside me, and I suddenly realized he is bigger than I.

What do I make of the transformation that has come about in our family room? Simply this: everyone needs to be close. Call it family, friendship, the church, salvation—we all need closeness—with each other, with God. If we do not have a place of closeness, we start going our own ways. That's why we need family, the church, a daily time with God. It took a new couch to remind me.

Susie is Coming

From the moment I got the letter, I lived with anticipation. Susie is coming. We will do this . . . I must show her this . . . I will fix . . . this . . . for dinner.

Susie had been a childhood friend. We had shared everything during first and second grade. Jumped rope together at recess. Ate our hot soup together at lunch. Sang together in a trio for second grade talent show. Shared our five-cent Popsicles that we bought when our school bus stopped at Mr. Gilmore's gas station on the way home after school each day. Explored wooded trails and dusty roads. Sat on her wide front porch and played paper dolls and dress-up. Finally at the end of an action-filled day, climbed into one of the two big double beds in the middle bedroom and drifted into sleep watching shadows from the fireplace flicker on the walls. We could count on warmth from that fireplace to dress by in the morning, because well before dawn, we knew Susie's mama would be up, feeding the fire with logs from the back porch.

Susie was a warm, happy thought. Not only did we share memories of childhood, but we shared the joy of reunion. Over the years, life had carried me to different parts of the country. We remembered the day, after almost fifteen years of having lost touch, when I walked into the corner drugstore of our little town in southern Alabama, called Susie's mother and found that Susie's husband owned the very drugstore in which I stood! It had been a joyful and tearful reunion—a reunion that has stretched now into almost twenty years.

Today as I walk through the house and think that in a few short weeks I will share it with Susie, I notice how much her presence is already here. I stop and look at the old black and white framed photo on my bookshelf. Susie and I are first graders, standing in front of her front porch steps, holding hands. She has black curls and I have long, dark braids. I see the wreath with a blue bow and white fluffy cotton bells Susie sent one Christmas to remind me of my cotton-picking days of long ago. My baskets in the family room are filled with *Southern Living* magazines. Susie has subscribed for me "to keep in touch with my southern roots." Two pictures hang on my kitchen wall with scenes of my past—a field of cotton and an old wooden ice cream freezer. Again, Susie's reminders of those simple things that made our past rich with memories.

Now we will build more memories. Susie's plane touches down and for several days, she moves with me through my world. Exploring the heart of Chicago. Tasting Chicago pizza. Tracing the places we've lived, the schools I've attended, the churches we've served. The stores where I shop. The streets where I walk. The schools our children attend. Even the parks where I relax. Through it all, we talk non-stop.

And when the whirlwind four days are over and we hug each other good-bye at Gate 7 of D concourse, I walk toward the car with a lump in my throat. I have been reminded of the bonds of friendship. I have also been reminded of a Friend who walks with me through all of my days. Oh that I would share the same anticipation and joy for Him!

CHAPTER SEVEN

Secrets of Tears

"You Were My Friend."

I came to you with my hurt
Like a child with a cut finger
Needing care
I brought it to you
Raw wound that it was
Not knowing
Exactly
Where it came from
Or what I needed.
I only knew the hurt.

You could have been my doctor.
  "Here, let me fix it for you."
You could have been my judge.
  "You should not feel that way."
You could have been my analyst.
  "The reason you feel this way is. . . ."

Instead
You were my friend.
You simply
Listened
And then you reached out
And
Took my pain
Picked it up as surely as
One carries another's load.
I heard my sorrow in your voice
Saw my tears in your eyes
Felt my grief in your hug.

I came to you wounded
And
I went from you whole.
You were my friend.

A Grope in the Dark

It is a grope in the dark, of sorts. I am not sure of direction this morning as I wait in a line of construction traffic. I am irritated over the traffic, yes, but also over the uncertainty. Ordered person that I am, I like my days planned in careful precision—everything making sense and fitting into the overall plan I've laid out for myself.

Why, then, this seeming detour—this part-time job at a local clothing store. The job seemed tailor-made for me— flexibility, low pressure, friendly . . . but still I wondered. At least, I thought it was. Why did I feel that it was so right for me to take on these part-time hours to help meet climbing college costs and miscellaneous expenses for a family growing toward college years? This new three-day work commitment did not exactly fit my long-range plan. It was not in my personal timetable. Try as I might, I could find no slot for it. It had simply come, attached with a peace of mind, and somehow I just knew it was right.

But today as I sit in muddled traffic, I am still trying to figure out why. I find myself tired before the day even begins. Trying to find reasons why is hard work. I glance to the list of errands lying on the seat beside me—all to be done by 9 A.M. Stamps are number one on the list. I do not know it, but this morning I will leave the post office with more than stamps.

True to the trend of the morning, there is another irritating wait in front of the stamp counter. I am fourth in line. From the corner of my eye, I see a woman in gray approaching slowly, cautiously. Then I see the white-tipped cane and I know it is all right to look. She cannot see me watching.

It seems she has come to the post office alone—no seeing eye dog, no human companion. She does not stop at the end of the line. To her, there is no end of the line. She feels her way straight down the middle, between counter and bodies, tapping slightly a child who had been playing happily in the open space but now, at the poke of a cane, scurries in fright to her mother. As though she has lost her sense of direction, the lady in gray halts uncertainly in no-man's-land. All six window clerks are busy, and the dozen or so of us witnessing the drama shift uneasily. We should be doing something but we don't know what to do. At least she is spared the embarrassment of knowing a dozen or so pairs of eyes are focused on her. "Next," the clerk calls from the farthest window.

The lady turns her head in the direction of the voice but moves straight ahead toward the marble wall. Someone from our waiting group rushes forward.

"Here, may I help you?" And a kind hand reaches out to lead her in the right direction. I have been touched, as surely as if that hand had reached out for me. I sense that a divine hand is doing the same for my current grope in the dark. *Lord, thank you for my eyes that sometimes see and sometimes don't.*

I buy my stamps and carefully direct myself out the door and down the post office steps. As I head across the street to my new part-time job, I am at peace with the fact that not everything in my life will always fall together in perfect sense. I have been reminded that even when I cannot see, there is always that invisible hand reaching out, guiding me in right directions.

"Darkness, My Friend?"

Heman the Ezrahite was having a bad day. He ended his musical lament (recorded in Psalm 88) with the words, "The darkness is my closest friend."

How depressing, I thought to myself on that bright spring day, so full of hope and anticipation. I closed my Bible on my psalm for the day and moved on to happier thoughts—the trip to Disney World with Jori's high-school choir. We would be boarding the bus in a matter of hours as chaperones for the tour. *How can darkness be a friend?* I pursued the question casually between final packing and a quick trip to the grocery store. Before the day was over, I would know.

The phone call came around noon. "Mother, all my tour money was stolen from my purse, taken right from my locker during lunch." The voice at the other end of the line sounded as if it were coming from a deep canyon somewhere. "What am I going to do? I have no money for the trip."

No money for the trip, I echoed her words in my mind. The reality was like some sinister plot waiting to be unraveled. I knew how hard Jori had worked and saved for her Chicago to Florida excursion. Now the money was gone. I had no idea what she would do for money. And in three short hours, the bus would head south.

I offered what meager comfort I could muster, assured her I would pray or run out to school to be with her, or do whatever I could. But my words were minus the hope. *How would we ever retrieve money stolen from a locker during lunch?*

I thought again about the psalm I had just read. This time I felt the darkness, but I did not feel it was a friend. It was an enemy that robbed high-school seniors of their hard-earned money and made mothers' hearts ache for their children's pain. *Why did life have to blot out the sun over my children's joy?* I asked myself.

Two hours later I walked past the scene of the crime. Outside, the Greyhound bus was being loaded for the trip south. But inside, all over the school—along the rows of lockers, taped on the walls—were green posters that read: "Choir member's tour money stolen. Please give your donation when the bucket comes by your classroom."

Halfway down the hall I met a tearful Jori. She was surrounded by her friends. "Mother, do you know what they did? They took an offering." We hugged each other and cried together.

As I stood in a circle with fifty-three high schoolers around me, listening to last minute instructions before we boarded the bus, I suddenly understood Heman the Ezrahite's strange combination of words. Jori stepped into the middle of the circle. "The last two hours have been pretty painful. But you all have shown me what Christian love is all about. And I want to thank you."

Pain, yes. But pain so that she would have the opportunity to see the love of Christ at work in her fellow classmates. Darkness, yes. But darkness so that mother and daughter alike would be reminded that hard times are sometimes the best times.

Perhaps Heman the Ezrahite was depressed when he wrote, "The darkness is my closest friend." But somehow I believe he recorded divine wisdom when he put the words "darkness" and "friend" together. For that day darkness truly had been our friend.

Message of Tears

I am touched today by the silent, yet forceful message of tears. I see them gather in the eyes of my friend as she shares with me a childhood trauma. Her lips quiver, and as the tears spill down her cheeks, I see what a tender heart she has. She unashamedly dries them with her napkin before they splash on her blueberry muffin. These tears are tears of remembering an illness that almost took her mom's life. I reach out and squeeze her hand. I can feel her tenderness. She cares deeply.

I am touched again today by the tears of my mother. She is visiting me. We have toured the fall foliage and seen the pumpkins in the fields, and drunk hot coffee. As we drive we remember laughter—the time one of us five children accidentally knocked down a leaf of the kitchen table and sent china and dinner flying in all directions. Mother laughed then as she laughs now at the memory.

Her laughter is contagious and genuine. I can see it in the tears that stream down her face.

"Grandma, who ever heard of someone laughing and crying at the same time?" one of my children had once remarked. *She does laugh and cry at the same time, so great are her celebrations of life,* I thought. These tears this morning show the depth of her joy.

Later as I read Luke 19, I am touched again by tears, tears of concern. God, the Creator of the universe in the form of human flesh, stopped on the dusty road outside of Jerusalem and cried for a city. His were tears of grief because he knew what was in store for the people who rejected God's love. I suspect that the tears flowed unashamedly that day too. He was with the Pharisees— the very ones who caused him grief. If he needed to impress anyone, it was the Pharisees. But he was not concerned with the strongman's image of power and control. He did not need to freeze his emotions and flex his spiritual muscles. Instead he cried, in the very presence of his enemies! I don't know and Scripture doesn't say, but perhaps those pious Jewish leaders whispered into their gray beards, "My how he cares!"

I think perhaps I need to cry more often—to weep for the love of friends the way the Ephesian elders did when they said good-bye to Paul at Miletus (Acts 20). Paul, too, was a man of tears. "I served the Lord with great humility and with tears . . . " (20:19) he said to them in his farewell speech. The elders were men of tears. "They all wept as they embraced him (Paul) and kissed him." (20:37). There they were, crying—grown men, leaders of the church. I need to cry for love, the way Timothy did when he thought of his mentor, Paul. "Recalling your tears," Paul said of Timothy, and "I long to see you so that I may be filled with joy," (2 Timothy 1:4).

Today as I remember tears, I remember my friend's tears of tenderness, my mother's tears of laughter, Jesus' tears of sorrow for sin, and Paul and his friends' tears of love. And I pray, *Lord, deliver me from a hard heart and dry eyes.* For it may be that sometimes my tears, too, speak far more than my words ever can.

Gentle Reminder

Interestingly enough, life's lessons are often learned in retrospect. I learn such a lesson when I talked with my parents.

"Remember Wendy Woodburn?" my mother asked. "She graduated the year before you. Died yesterday of complications from pneumonia. Very suddenly. I just saw her last Saturday in the drug store."

If there had been anything I remember hearing again and again in high school, it was, "God's way is the best way." I believed it, and yet, I was not always sure.

Sometimes it seemed like Wendy Woodburn's way was the best way. I admired her, envied her good looks, and the boys who vied constantly for her attention. Wendy never lacked for dates, money, or opportunities. I often thought with great discontent, *If only I could live in a house like Wendy's.*

Wendy had it all, or at least it seemed—head majorette for the band, soloist for the choir, queen of homecoming, center of most conversations, parties, and lunchroom cliques. Whatever she did, it seemed she did it with smoothness and grace. And she always seemed to do it right.

Except for her faith. Everyone knew she had none. But it never seemed to be a limiting factor; in fact, if anything, her free-and-easy, no-faith life always seemed to work in her favor. Whatever she did seemed to prosper, even without God in her life.

No wonder I had trouble when I read in Psalm 1 that only the righteous would prosper. As far as I could tell, Wendy was not righteous and still prospered. I aimed for righteousness but certainly did not consider myself prosperous in contrast to Wendy. Little did I know that thirty years later I would gain perspective.

"Wendy literally self-destructed," my dad went on. "I visited her once in the hospital just before she died. Pneumonia was not the cause."

I heard what my dad was saying. I had known in recent years of Wendy's spiral downward, but I had carried with me my high-school illusions of Wendy as the person who had it all. And in my adult skepticism, which sometimes momentarily clouded my perspective, I would think of Wendy and ask myself again, *Why do the wicked prosper?*

Today as I read Wendy's obituary in the newspaper mother has sent from home, I am reminded of Psalm 1 and the wicked who are "like chaff that the wind blows away." I also remember that the godly are "like a tree . . . whose leaf does not wither." I sadly fold the newspaper clipping and file it away in my memento box of people and places I have known.

Today I have a new respect for the true meaning of the word *prosper* from God's point of view. And strangely enough, I suddenly realize that I, not Wendy, was the prosperous one, even way back there in high school.

CHAPTER EIGHT

Secrets of Joy

"I Am Loved."

I am loved.
You look at me with eyes filled with compassion
Tenderly wipe my tears when I cry
Shelter me from the cold blasts that blow against my face
Give me resources when I am emptied of my own.

I am loved.
Your arms go round me when I am weak
Your voice calms me when I fear
Your smile warms me when I am cold.

And I say to myself as I go my way each day
My Heavenly Father
Notices
Loves
Cares about me.

The Worshiper

Dark comes early on winter evenings here in this thousand-year-old walled city of Zofingen, Switzerland. We have strolled the cobblestoned streets, enjoying sights, sounds, and smells. As in most European cities, the cathedral in the center of town dominates the scene. It rises before us now—stately, gothic, and somber in the evening dusk. We are on our way home to dinner, but we are interrupted by the edifice before us. Like a magnet, the high, ornate door draws us. We step into the dim sacredness.

From the front of the long, stone nave, a voice rises and falls in evening prayer. We see a kneeling form at the altar. Thoughts of dinner fade. We slip silently into a pew, bow in our own insignificance. We are not humbled so much by towering gothic arches and stained glass windows as by the voice at prayer.

I do not understand his language, but it is as if I understand his heart. He speaks a language of love, not a recital of memorized words. He is talking warmly and personally to his friend. He does not plead. He does not beg. He does not whine. His voice is confident, genuine, full of admiration and appreciation. It is as if he is applauding God.

We continue to sit in silent contemplation, captivated by this evening prayer. I think perhaps he is in the praise portion of his private vespers. Entreaty will come next. *How often do we pray without petition?* I ask myself. But his canticle of praise continues. I sense his joy in every word. His plea never comes—no cry for mercy, grace, peace, daily bread. It is as if he already has all he needs. His God is more than a mere bread-giver.

"Time to go?" my friend whispers after our prolonged silence. I nod silently and we move quietly back toward the front door.

I know the answer, but I whisper the question anyway. "What was he saying?"

"His whole prayer, he was thanking God," my Switzerland hostess responds.

I reflect as we walk through the narrow streets and pass under the thick arches of the city gate. *When was the last time I simply thanked my heavenly Father? How long since my prayers were full of praise rather than full of petition? Do I applaud God because of what he can do for me or simply for who he is?*

Soberly I go home to dinner. And I wonder as I eat my cheese fondue whether that voice in the cathedral might still be praising.

The Song That Preached a Sermon

For better, for worse." I've often thought of these words in relation to marriage, but this morning the phrase takes on a whole new meaning.

The sultry August air forces itself through the high windows bordering the gymnasium-turned-sanctuary. Three giant floor fans redirect the steamy air over several hundred worshipers who have gathered here in the heart of Chicago's black community. Although my husband, Mark, son Nick, and I are definitely the white minority, we are greeted with open arms and warm smiles. We are immediately caught up into the rhythmic praises.

And indeed praise does flow here in this house of worship among the orange plastic chairs, snare drums, and paint that peels from the walls. The joy that the drums and the organ beat out in rhythm is inescapable. The joy claps and sways and jumps. It weaves its way through the songs and shows up on the faces around us. Joy is so full here in this place of worship that it bursts the old wineskins (Mark 2:22)—my liturgy, my traditions, my rigidity, my inhibitions. It overflows—this joyous celebration of God's love. I respond naturally. I sing like I've never sung before.

This is truly a house of praise, but also a house of remembrance. "This do in remembrance of me." On the communion table, a white vase holds red and white silk flowers and a pair of forgotten sunglasses rests stems up. I smile at the paradox between forgotten sunglasses and remembered blood. It was, in fact, that very blood that linked forever the human and the divine, closed the gap. Perhaps forgotten sunglasses are the perfect example, although I am fairly certain they are on the communion table this morning by mistake more than by design.

The message calls me to remember, not only the blood and the cross, but also deliverance; it calls me to remember the fiery furnace and the test of faithfulness. I can almost see the flames leaping. Hope is almost gone for the three Hebrew youth. "But there was a fourth man . . . Who was that fourth man?" the preacher asks. The organ swells, voices raise in one united response. "That fourth man was the Son of God." I am carried from bondage in Egypt to a wrestling match with an angel by the ford of the Jabbok, to the mouth of lions, to the sword of the Amorites. Each time the preacher asks, "Who was that fourth man?" And each time I respond with the crowd, "That fourth man was the Son of God."

But this house of worship is even more—it's a house of surrender. "I'm yours Lord, everything I am. Everything I've got. Everything I'm not." I sway and sing with the choir. Suddenly, I am stopped short. *It is one thing to give to* the Lord what I am. It is quite another to give to him all that I'm not. I give him my best, but my worst? God is not worthy of my worst.

As the choir continues to sing, probably for the first time in my life, I consciously surrender my best and my worst. God is big enough to handle both.

I go out into the hot August sunshine at the end of the three hour service, with a new sense of God's grace. His love for me includes all I am *and* all I'm not. I leave this place of worship with renewed hope.

Celebration of Joy

 The fog that surrounds us is thick and depressing. It has followed Jori and me for several days, shuttering in our little green Opal as it chugs the narrow, winding auto paths near southern Germany's Bodensee. Cold, damp nothingness is beginning to move inside. We find it hard to muster much enthusiasm for our planned trip to Bavaria.

But this morning, we take to the road again, not willing to waste my two remaining days in Germany, sights or no sights. We have little hope of seeing the countryside.

We ride for several hours in gray monotony, carried along only by lively conversation inside the car. I can tell we are climbing in elevation. The little green Opal grinds its engine and I shift to a lower gear. As far as we can tell, we are solitary companions with the road. There is no world beyond, only fog.

Suddenly, we blink, and the world is transformed into an ancient hilltop village, gray cobblestone streets, and white church spires, which tower toward the blue. There is not a trace of fog.

We have not only entered sunlight, but we have also entered a celebration this Sabbath morning. Through the cobblestone streets come the worshipers; first the clergy in flowing white, followed by acolytes and choir, robed in purple and gold and carrying flags and a large Christian cross. Jubilant villagers march to the toll of the bells, making their way up to worship in the church.

I stop the car and turn off the engine. What a glorious and sacred moment! I remember the Old Testament psalmists who led the way into the temple with grand processions and songs of ascent.

And I wonder, sitting there in that tiny German hilltop town, where I lost my joy in worship. Far too often, corporate worship is a dry, meaningless ritual, which I perform flawlessly between 9:30 and 10:30 every Sunday morning. Or private worship becomes a gloomy introspection that leaves me feeling depressed and discouraged.

When Nehemiah brought physical and spiritual restoration to Jerusalem after a hundred years of exile, the people gathered to worship. Scribe Ezra dusted off the Book of the Law of Moses and read it aloud to the people from daybreak till noon. When the people heard the Word, they began to cry, as well they might. They had forgotten the God of their covenant for hundreds of years. In the midst of their weeping, Nehemiah gave an interesting command. "Do not weep . . . go and enjoy choice food and sweet drinks . . . this day is sacred to our LORD . . . for the joy of the Lord is your strength" (Neh. 8:9–10).

If today, God could move in among both our

corporate and our private worship, I wonder if he might not say, "Lay aside your guilt and despair. In your worship, plan processions of praise, consciously choose joy. I have set you free." Surely that would be enough for a victory parade through golden rays of the morning sun in a tiny German town.

Forever Young

Seventy-two years old isn't exactly young, I think to myself as I look into my dad's face and listen to yet another of his stories from one of the hospitals, prisons or nursing homes he visits in his rounds as church visitation pastor. *He really should start slowing down.* I remember seeing the figure "600" for last year's hospital calls recorded in his visitation log. And that figure didn't even include the nursing homes and prisons.

This afternoon Dad hangs his coat and hat in the front hall closet, returns to the kitchen and tells us his story. His eyes are alive and snappy, his smile, wide. His words seem as though they can hardly wait to spill out.

It had been morning rounds as usual at Lancaster General Hospital. Listening. Comforting. Reading. Praying. An elderly woman with a hip replacement. A man with back surgery. A church member's neighbor, in for testing. A young father dying from cancer.

The final visit had been the toughest of all. How do you answer the "Whys" of a dad in the prime of life who will never live to see his sons play baseball? What can one say about the frightening valley of the shadow that lies just beyond?

Daddy listened, read from the Psalms, prayed, then quietly left. There were more visits to make at the other hospital across town. He'd best be on his way if he hoped to get all the calls made before noon.

Not one to frequent coffee shops or even spend time drinking coffee, it was an unusual move for Daddy to turn into the hospital coffee shop on his way to the car.

"Not sure why I did it except I had this sudden urge for a cup of coffee." Dad said it with the intrigue of a mystery writer.

As he sat sipping hot coffee, planning in his mind his next four stops, he heard his name being paged. "Reverend Hollinger. Please pick up the nearest courtesy phone."

It was the church secretary who had just received a call at church from Tom, the young cancer patient on third floor.

"If you can find Pastor Hollinger, please have him come back to my room as soon as possible."

In no time, Dad was back on third floor, sitting between the beds of two young cancer victims. Tom's roommate reached out his thin hand for Dad.

"I couldn't help but overhear your conversation with Tom. I want what you were talking about. Please tell me how."

And there in west wing of Lancaster General Hospital, a seventy-two-year-old visitation pastor and two young cancer patients bowed before the throne of heaven and a new son was welcomed home!

I felt as though I was right there in the throne room, bowing with them. Mother and I wiped the tears. As for Daddy, his face shone, maybe a little like the face of Moses when he'd been with God. I noticed, strangely enough, how few wrinkles Dad had, even when he smiled.

No wonder, I thought to myself. *Dad is involved in new birth.* I patted him on his hand. *No wonder he seems forever young.*

Story completed, Dad heads out into the afternoon to mow the yard and tend his small garden.

"Those who wait [even in hospital coffee shops!] on the Lord, shall renew their strength . . ." Today I have seen visual proof. So much for worrying that Daddy really should be slowing down. Today I've changed my mind.